Left-brain Puzzles

hinkler

Published by Hinkler Books Pty Ltd
45–55 Fairchild Street
Heatherton Victoria 3202 Australia
www.hinkler.com

hinkler

Cover design: Sam Grimmer
Internal design: Book Creation and Hinkler Design Studio
Cover images: Book Creation or Shutterstock.com
Prepress: Graphic Print Group

Printed and bound in China

978 1 4889 3529 9

Left-brain Puzzles Introduction

Dhave you ever had to whip out your phone to calculate a 20% tip, or to figure out who owes what when splitting the bill? Do you struggle to construct the perfect sentence to get your point across? Or perhaps you want to improve your crossword, Sudoku or chess-playing skills? All these abilities depend on the left-hand hemisphere of your brain – where words and numbers are processed, and the centre of problem-solving, mental arithmetic, deductive and intuitive reasoning, logic and lateral thinking. 'Use it or lose it' applies just as much to your mind as it does to your muscles – the more you practice a particular activity, the better you'll become at it. So, if you want to improve any (or all) of these abilities, the best way to do it is to train the area of your brain responsible for those abilities – the left hemisphere. This collection includes everything you need to do just that!

Deductive Puzzles is designed to help you hone your problem-solving, lateral-thinking, and word-processing abilities. Its puzzles will challenge your left brain by asking you to find solutions based on patterns, known facts or principles, and logic and reasoning.

Numeric Puzzles is for those who want to brush up on their mental maths – here you'll find number-based games and challenges designed to improve the speed and accuracy of your mental calculations. You'll be amazed at how much easier mathematical problems become after a bit of practice!

Just like training your body, training your mind is most effective when you actually enjoy doing it. That's why this collection of puzzles is designed to be fun, even addictive! You won't even realize you're breaking a mental sweat! Every puzzle is rated by difficulty on a scale of 1–10 stars, so you can choose to tackle them in their current order, or start with the one-star challenges and work your way up to the ten-star challenges. Each puzzle comes with its own time limit too, to keep you on your toes! But if you get stuck, there's no need to worry – answers are included at the back of each section.

You can power through these puzzles on your own, or start a game with friends and family – however you prefer to train your brain and no matter what your level of ability, there is plenty of fun brain training in here for you!

CONTENTS

Deductive Puzzles

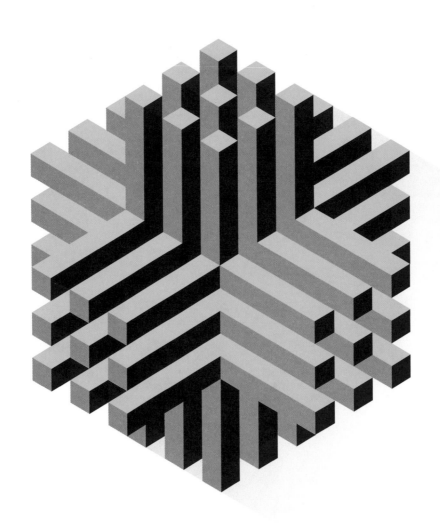

eductive Puzzles is a brand-new, user-friendly tour around the world of puzzles for those who get a kick out of getting the right answer.

Everything in here is all black or white, right or wrong, so there'll be no arguments—apart from whose turn it is to try the next puzzle!

Deduction is a form of logic that can be used to find the solution to a problem based on a set of known facts or principles. A simple example of deductive reasoning is as follows:

1. Only birds have feathers.
2. An ostrich has feathers.
3. Therefore, an ostrich must be a bird.

If the first two statements are known to be facts, then the third statement can be deduced from them.

Deductive reasoning is a skill powered by the left-hand side of the brain. The puzzles in this section have been specifically designed to train your left brain by triggering problem-solving, deductive and intuitive reasoning, logic and lateral-thinking.

Nuances of logic can be surprisingly subtle. For example, suppose we asked you to describe whether the statement "Some birds have black feathers" is always, sometimes, or never true. Many people are tempted to choose "sometimes" because the statement appears conditional. However, the correct answer is "always" because there are always some birds somewhere in the world that have black feathers. What if we asked you to describe the truth of the statement "Some birds are ugly"? In this instance, none of the three answers can be chosen because the statement is a matter of opinion and there's no right or wrong answer. These distinctions, subtle though they are, form the basis for some branches of philosophy.

So if you're dying to test out your own powers of deduction, where to head next? You could go straight through this section tackling each one as it comes. However, if you want to ease yourself in more gently, look for our special grading system. Each puzzle is rated from 1 to 10 stars. Low numbers of stars indicate that the puzzle shouldn't deter you too long. An 8-, 9- or 10-star problem means you're likely to be taxed to your limit. Furthermore, there are time limits to keep an eye on, just to increase the tension that little bit more.

Every question is numbered and has its answer clearly marked in the back of the section. But be sure to try all avenues before resorting to the solutions—things are not always what they seem at first!

By the end of this section, you'll be a master of deducing right from wrong. And that's the truth. ✪

—David Bodycombe

1 DIFFICULTY ✪✪✪✪✪☆☆☆☆☆   ⏱ **5** Minutes

If you think tic-tac-toe is boring, try this interesting variation. The aim of the game is to avoid winning—in other words, if you get three of your symbol in a horizontal, vertical, or diagonal line, you lose the game.

In the sample game shown, it is O's turn. Can you see which of the four possibilities (A, B, C, or D) will lead to a guaranteed win?

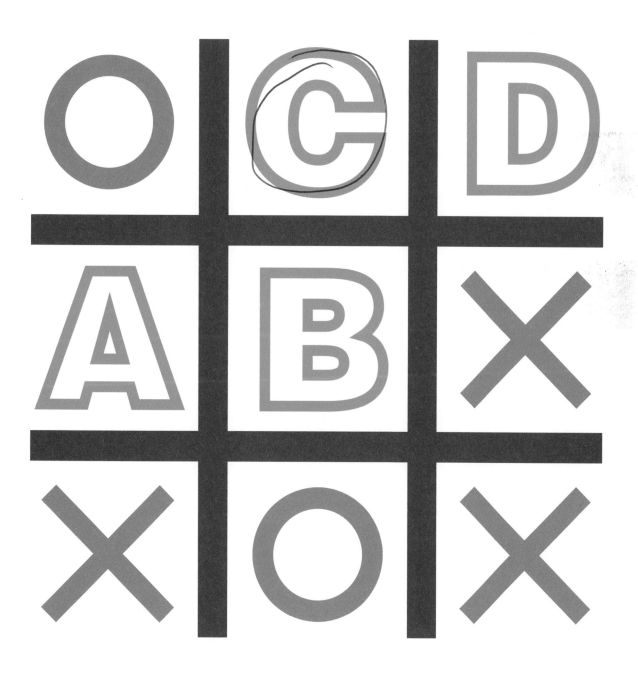

2 DIFFICULTY ✪✪✪✪✪✪✪☆☆☆☆  **7 Minutes**

Can you crack the safe? First decide which of the 14 statements given are false, then shade out the areas on the combination lock that are labeled with the letters of those false statements (so if you think statement A is false, shade out area A). The remaining lit segments will give you the digital combination required.

Hint: three of the statements are false.

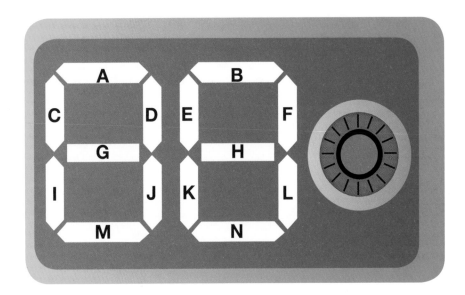

A. The upper number in a fraction is the numerator.
B. The ratio of a circle's circumference to its diameter is called pi.
C. A league is the term for a nautical mile.
D. Euclid wrote a famous work on geometry.
E. The Roman numeral for 500 is D.
F. An irrational number cannot be expressed as a fraction.
G. The longest side of a right-angled triangle is the hypotenuse.
H. Andrew Wiles famously proved Fermat's last theorem.
I. Integral and differential are types of calculus.
J. Hexadecimal is the number system for counting in groups of 12.
K. A reflex angle has between 90 and 180 degrees.
L. A heptagon has seven sides.
M. A perfect number is equal to the sum of all of its factors.
N. Originally, a myriad was equal to 10,000.

3 DIFFICULTY ✪✪✪✪✪☆☆☆☆☆ ⏰ **3** Minutes

Each block is equal to the sum of the two numbers beneath it.
Can you find all the missing numbers?

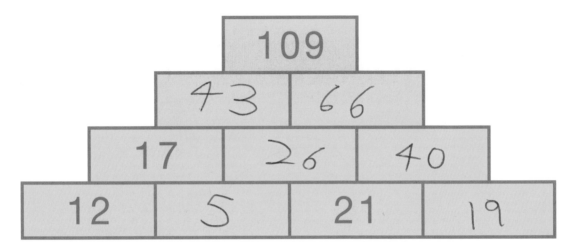

4 DIFFICULTY ✪✪✪✪☆☆☆☆☆☆ ⏰ **6** Minutes

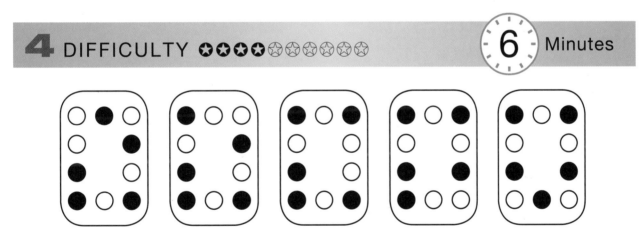

Which shape below comes next in the above sequence?

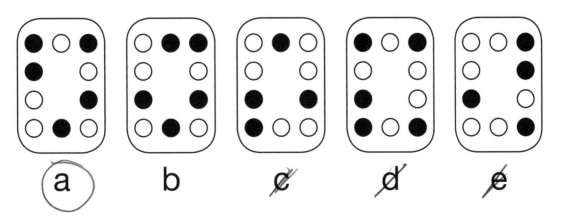

a   b   c̸   d̸   e̸

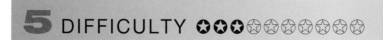

Can you fit these numbers into the grid? One number has already been inserted to help you get started.

135

4225
1767463

3 DIGITS	5 DIGITS	7 DIGITS
~~135~~	18915	~~1767463~~
~~208~~	~~21266~~	2096913
424	~~24437~~	~~2678374~~
650	~~32791~~	~~3235488~~
	~~43420~~	4937541
4 DIGITS	55159	4965907
1543	~~61605~~	5244243
2246	79937	5997845
~~4225~~	~~82314~~	~~6583226~~
5890	90556	6796588
~~6134~~		~~7216860~~
~~7979~~	**6 DIGITS**	~~8822997~~
8199	~~130471~~	9124965
~~9484~~	530395	9721305
	766860	
	~~897030~~	

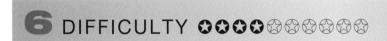 

6 DIFFICULTY ★★★★☆☆☆☆☆☆ **6** Minutes

Each row and column contains the same numbers and signs, but they are arranged in a different order each time. Find the correct order to arrive at the final totals shown.

2	+	6	x	3	–	4	= 20
							= 10
							= 16
							= 17
=		=		=		=	
8		13		2		24	

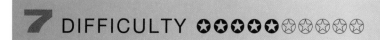

7 DIFFICULTY ●●●●●☆☆☆☆☆  5 Minutes

Make a calculation totaling the figure on the right by inserting the four mathematical operators (+, −, ÷, x) between the numbers shown.

They can be inserted in any order, and one of them has been used twice.

| 2 | 3 | 8 | 7 | 5 | 4 | = | 6 |

8 DIFFICULTY ●●●●●☆☆☆☆☆  8 Minutes

Five hopefuls brought their animals to the county fair. Can you figure out whose animal won which prize, and what kind of animal it was?

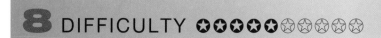

	Pig	Goat	Calf	Chicken	Sheep	1st	2nd	3rd	4th	5th	Ned	Flo	Mavis	Bob	Jack
Norbert															
Tizzy															
Spot															
Guffy															
Pong															
Ned															
Flo															
Mavis															
Bob															
Jack															
1st															
2nd															
3rd															
4th															
5th															

1. Flo's chicken was beaten by only one other animal.
2. Spot the pig wasn't last, but he didn't win.
3. Jack's calf came in 5th—one place behind Bob's Guffy.
4. The owner of Norbert the sheep isn't a woman.
5. Tizzy placed better than Pong.

9 DIFFICULTY ✪✪✪✪✪✪✩✩✩✩ | **1** Minute

Study these shapes for one minute, then see if you can answer the questions on the next page.

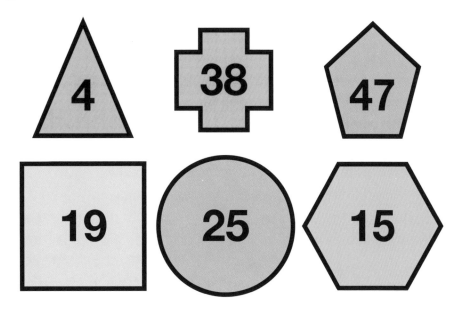

10 DIFFICULTY ✪✪✪✪✪✩✩✩✩✩ | **5** Minutes

To continue the logic, what time should it say on the sixth clock in this sequence?

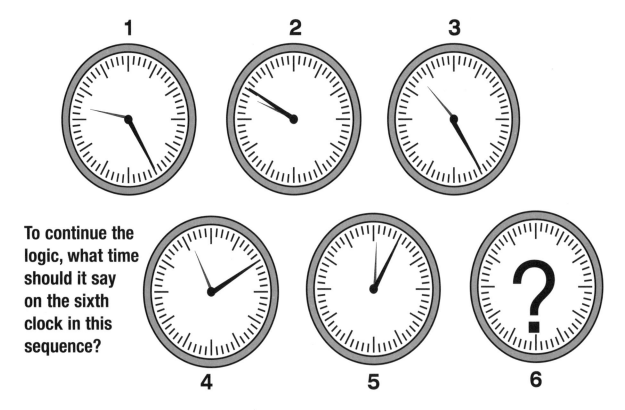

[9] DIFFICULTY ✪✪✪✪✪☆☆☆☆☆   **3** Minutes

Can you answer these questions about the puzzle on the previous page without looking back?

1. How many shapes have odd numbers?
2. Which three numbers will total a fourth number shown?
3. What is the total when you multiply the number on the blue shape by that on the shape directly above the blue shape?
4. Which shapes have even numbers?
5. What is the total of the numbers on the green shapes?
6. What is the total when you add the number on the pink shape to that on the circle, then subtract this total from the number on the pentagon?
7. Which two shapes of the same color are horizontally next to one another?
8. What is the total of the three numbers in the shapes on the top row?

11 DIFFICULTY ✪✪✪✪☆☆☆☆☆☆   **7** Minutes

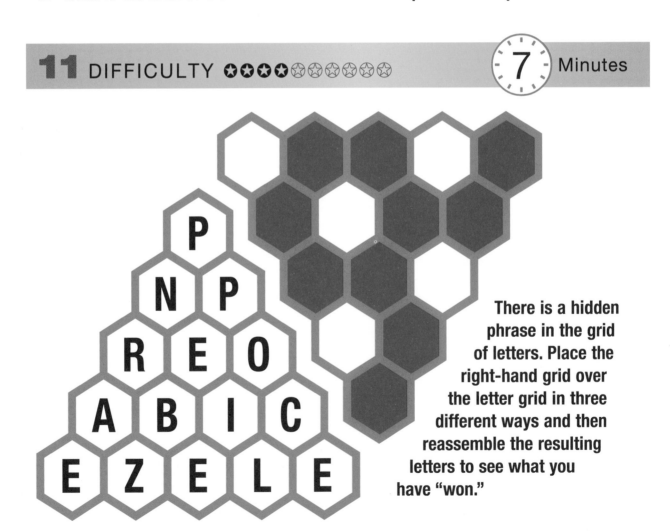

There is a hidden phrase in the grid of letters. Place the right-hand grid over the letter grid in three different ways and then reassemble the resulting letters to see what you have "won."

12 DIFFICULTY ✪✪✪✪✪✪✪☆☆☆   30 Minutes

You'll be flying high if you solve this numeropic. Use the rules below to help you understand how to complete this puzzle.

How to do a numeropic:

Along each row or column, there are numbers that indicate how many blocks of black squares are in a line. For example, "3, 4, 5" indicates that from left to right or top to bottom, there is a group of three black squares, then a group of four black squares, then another group of five black squares.

Each block of black squares on the same line must have at least one white square between it and the next block of black squares. Blocks of black squares may or may not have a number of white squares before and after them.

It is sometimes possible to determine which squares will be black without reference to other lines or columns. It is helpful to put a small dot in a square you know will be empty.

Column clues (top to bottom):

				7	6	6	4											2			2								
8	8	8	3	4	4	2	4		4		3		2		1		4		7	2	2	1	1						
1	1	2	5	4	3	2	2	4	1	4	4	2	4	1	4	1	3	9	8	1	5	3	3	4	4	6	7	8	
8	2	3	4	1	1	2	3	1	2	4	8	3	8	3	8	3	8	5	6	6	5	1	4	4	3	3	2	2	1
1	2	5	7	7	7	7	7	11	11	6	2	2	2	3	3	4	5	1	1	1	1	1	1	2	2	2	3	4	5
2	1	1	1	1	1	1	1	1	2	2	2	2	2	3	4	5	5	6	5	6	5	6	5	6	5	4	3	3	2	3

Row clues (left of each row):

Row	Clues
1	5 1
2	7 2
3	9 10
4	12 6 1
5	13 3 2
6	16 4 3
7	7 6 5 5
8	4 5 6
9	2 6 7
10	7 4 1 8
11	10 7 3 3
12	3 4 2
13	8
14	9 4 3 11
15	7 8 11
16	5 4 3 10
17	3 8 9 1
18	1 4 3 8 3
19	8 7 4
20	1 4 5 6
21	4 3 4 2
22	10 1
23	10 1 1
24	9 1 1
25	9 1 1 1 1
26	8 10
27	6 12
28	4 15 1
29	1 21
30	30

13 DIFFICULTY ★★★★★★☆☆☆☆ ④ Minutes

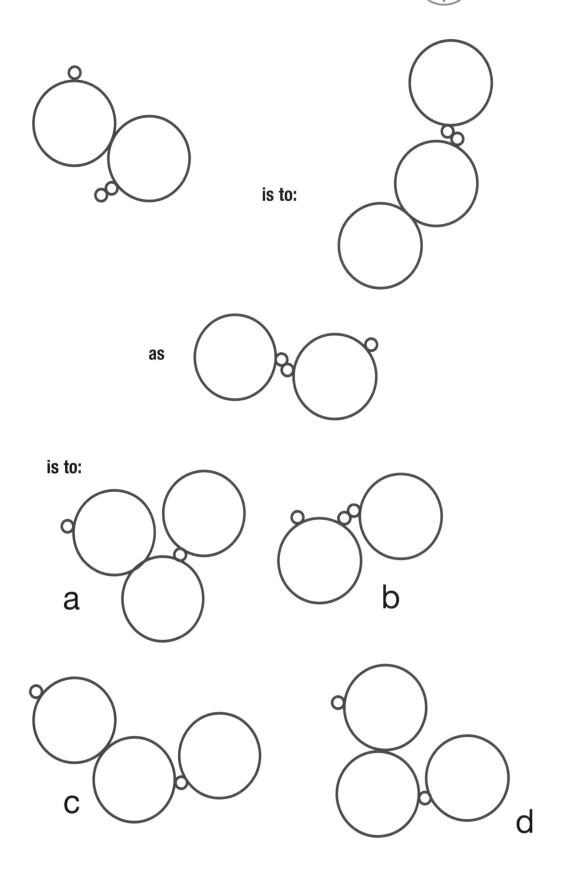

is to:

as

is to:

a

b

c

d

14 DIFFICULTY ●●●☆☆☆☆☆☆☆   ⊘ 2 Minutes

In what way are the start and end of each of these six times identical?

9:57	8:23
1:32	11:25
9:13	2:48

15 DIFFICULTY ●●●●●☆☆☆☆☆   ⊘ 5 Minutes

Place the remaining pieces in the grid so that:
* each row and column has two red and two yellow squares, and
* no row or column has two of the same digit.

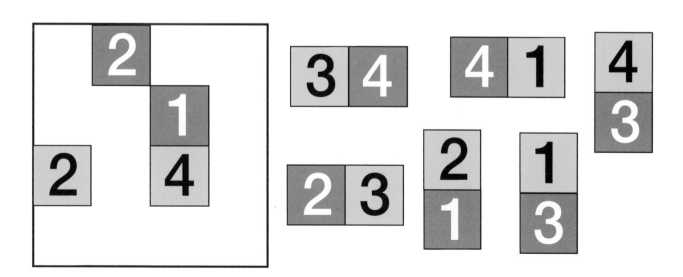

16 DIFFICULTY ●●●●○○○○○○

③ Minutes

Which of the four boxed figures (a, b, c, or d) completes the set?

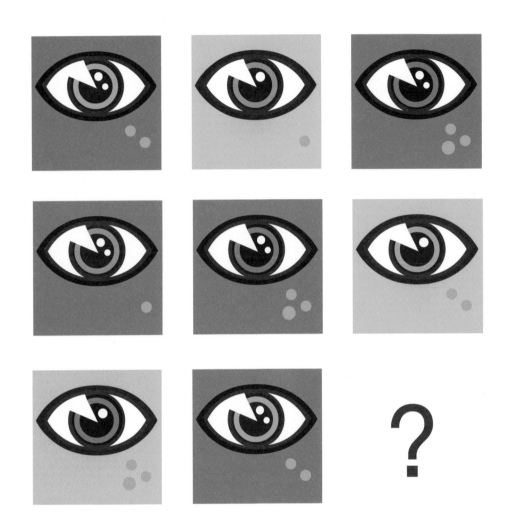

?

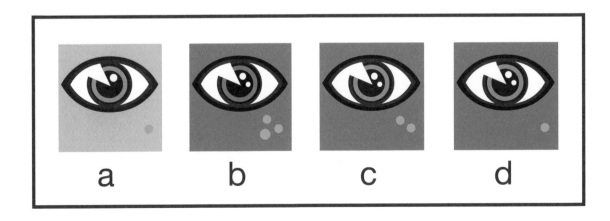

a   b   c   d

17 DIFFICULTY ✪✪✪✪✪✪☆☆☆☆  **8** Minutes

Try to get from the top left red square to the bottom right red square by making a series of calculations. You must always move from each square to an adjacent one and may not move diagonally.

8	÷	0	=	8	÷	2
−	1	=	9	÷	1	=
9	+	3	=	3	x	4
=	0	x	6	−	7	+
6	=	2	=	8	=	3
÷	2	=	4	=	8	−
1	=	3	x	9	+	3
=	3	x	2	÷	0	=
6	÷	3	=	2	=	8

18 DIFFICULTY ✪✪✪✪☆☆☆✩☆✩

⏱ **3** Minutes

The number 123987 appears just once in this grid and occurs in a straight line, running either backward or forward in a horizontal, vertical, or diagonal direction. Can you locate it?

9	3	2	1	7	3	1	2	3	8	9	7
7	8	2	2	8	9	1	2	3	9	8	2
1	3	1	7	3	2	2	2	2	9	3	1
9	2	2	8	3	1	3	9	1	8	2	2
7	8	3	1	2	3	7	7	7	3	1	3
8	7	9	3	2	1	8	8	9	2	8	9
3	1	7	7	9	3	9	1	1	7	8	7
2	2	8	9	3	3	7	2	2	3	2	8
1	2	3	9	2	2	3	8	3	2	7	7
7	1	8	1	3	9	1	9	1	1	8	3
8	3	1	2	3	7	9	8	7	3	9	2
9	7	1	2	3	8	7	9	3	2	1	1

19 DIFFICULTY ⭐⭐⭐⭐⭐☆☆☆☆☆ — 5 Minute

Each block is equal to the sum of the two numbers beneath it. Can you find all the missing numbers?

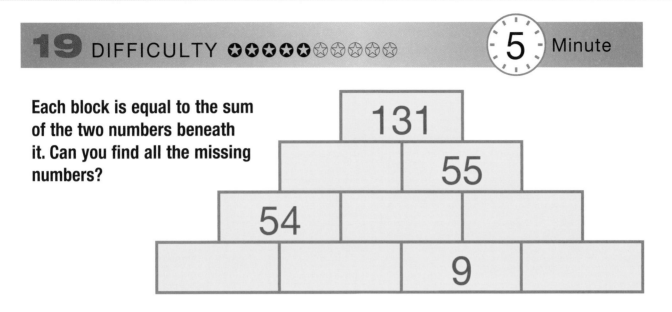

20 DIFFICULTY ⭐⭐⭐⭐⭐⭐☆☆☆☆ — 10 Minute

Take the cards to the left of the grid and place them so that each horizontal row and vertical column contains a joker plus four aces of different suits, and each shape (shown by the thick lines) also contains a joker plus four aces of different suits. Some cards are already in place.

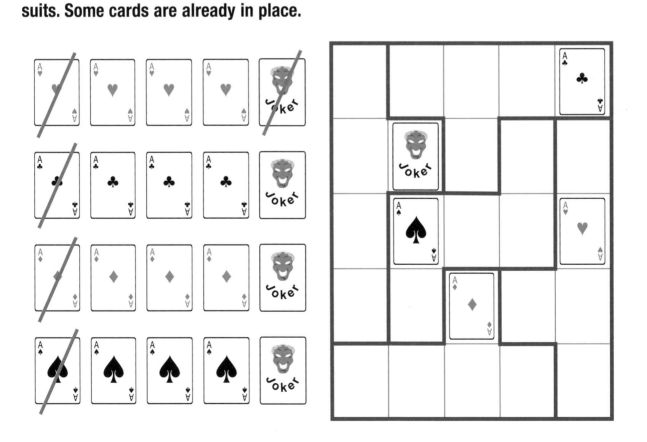

21 DIFFICULTY ⭐⭐⭐✩✩✩✩✩✩✩ ③ Minutes

Make a calculation totaling the figure on the right by inserting the four mathematical operators (+, −, ÷, x) between the numbers shown.

They can be inserted in any order, and one of them has been used twice.

| 9 | | 3 | | 6 | | 2 | | 4 | | 5 | = | 10 |

22 DIFFICULTY ⭐⭐⭐⭐⭐✩✩✩✩✩ ⑤ Minutes

Given that scales a and b balance perfectly, how many circles are needed to balance scale c?

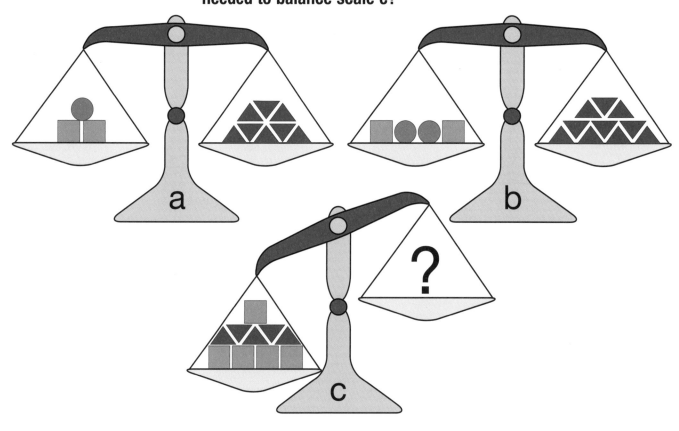

Which of these configurations is the odd one out?

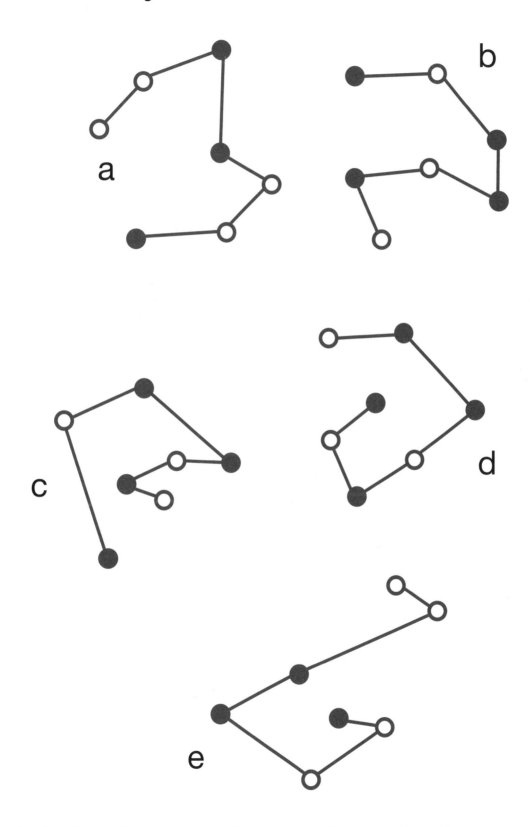

MINDW🧠RKS BRAIN TRAINING

24 DIFFICULTY ✪✪✪✪✪☆☆☆☆☆ ⑥ Minutes

Which of the four boxed figures (a, b, c, or d) completes the set?

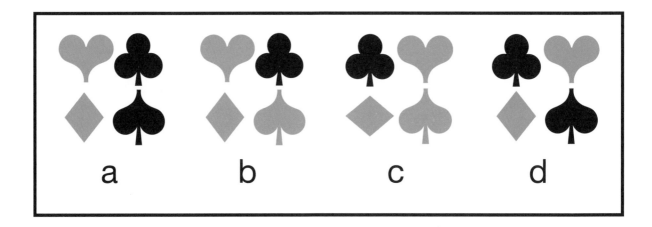

a   b   c   d

25 DIFFICULTY ●●●☆☆☆☆☆☆☆   5 Minutes

Can you fit these numbers into the grid? One number has already been inserted to help you get started.

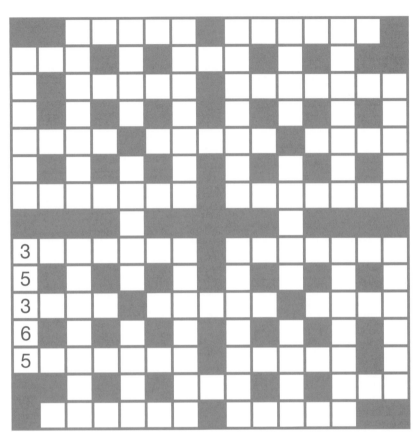

3 DIGITS	5 DIGITS	7 DIGITS
139	12968	1365903
226	13152	2239753
693	27856	2845686
809	~~35365~~	3368287
	42842	4653504
4 DIGITS	56922	4720952
1993	60983	5521661
2476	72776	5871164
3465	89116	6960242
4368	91309	7638663
5677		7710110
6107	**6 DIGITS**	8218369
7456	320730	9202897
9397	442282	9465268
	616937	
	886039	

26 DIFFICULTY ✪✪✪✪✪✪✪✩✩✩✩ ⏱ 8 Minutes

Five models each wore one of five items by five designers on the catwalk. Can you figure out each model's last name and which item, by which designer, each wore?

1. Ms. Jones didn't wear Vergucci, carry a bag, or wear gloves or blue.
2. The pink hat wasn't Fundi or Tom Buick, and Kate didn't wear it.
3. Naomi Taylor didn't wear gloves or shoes.
4. The Vergucci bag wasn't red.
5. Manon works for Armande, which doesn't make hats or gloves.
6. Jody wore all black but not Canale, and she didn't wear a coat.
7. Miss Dupris wore gold but not by Fundi or Armande, and she didn't wear gloves.
8. Ms. Briant wore Canale.
9. Tom Buick's collection was all blue.

	Jones	Dupris	Heaton	Taylor	Briant	Tom Buick	Vergucci	Canale	Fundi	Armande	Gloves	Hat	Bag	Shoes	Coat	Red	Blue	Pink	Gold	Black
Jody																				
Kate																				
Naomi																				
Emma																				
Manon																				
Red																				
Blue																				
Pink																				
Gold																				
Black																				
Gloves																				
Hat																				
Bag																				
Shoes																				
Coat																				
Tom Buick																				
Vergucci																				
Canale																				
Fundi																				
Armande																				

27 DIFFICULTY ✪✪✪✪✪✪✩✩✩✩✩ ⏱ 5 Minutes

Which pentagon from the selection below should replace the question mark?

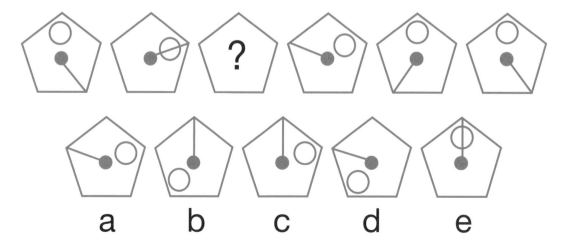

a b c d e

28 DIFFICULTY ★★★★★☆☆☆☆☆

Here's a very simple but effective game. Take 15 coins (it doesn't matter how they are arranged). Two players take turns picking up one, two, or three coins. Play continues until there are no coins left in the pile. The winner is the person who ends up with an odd number of coins.

Play the game a few times and see if you can figure out a winning strategy. The player who goes first always has the advantage, if he or she knows how to use it properly! For a variation, try starting with 13 coins.

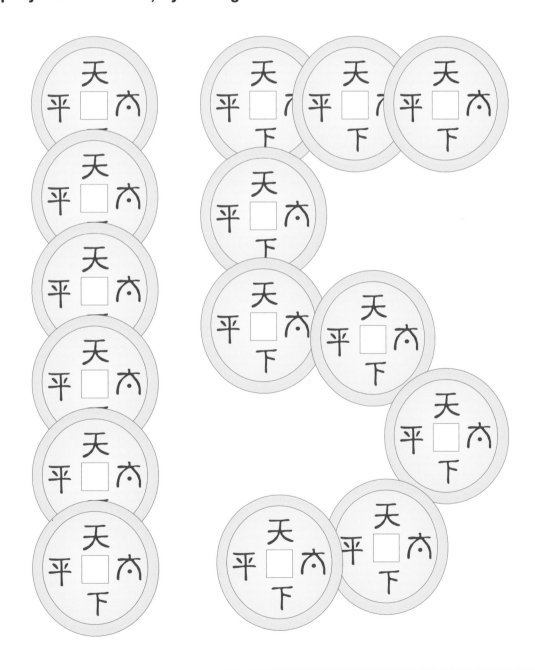

29 DIFFICULTY ✪✪✪✪✪✪☆☆☆☆☆ (5) Minutes

Given that scales a and b balance perfectly, how many gooseberries are needed to balance scale c?

30 DIFFICULTY ★★★★★☆☆☆☆☆  3 Minutes

What number comes next?

49, 62, 70, 77, 91, 101, 103, ?

31 DIFFICULTY ★★★★☆☆☆☆☆☆  4 Minutes

Which number is the odd one out?

7141 9187
3025 6140
8164 5149
2079 4193

32 DIFFICULTY ●●●●○○○○○○ (4) Minutes

Each row and column contains the same numbers and signs, but they are arranged in a different order each time. Find the correct order to arrive at the final totals shown.

5	+	4	x	2	–	7	=	11
							=	13
							=	4
							=	25
=		=		=		=		
16		6		7		17		

33 DIFFICULTY ✪✪✪✪✪✩✩✩✩✩ **4** Minutes

The number 246135 appears just once in this grid and occurs in a straight line, running either backward or forward in a horizontal, vertical, or diagonal direction. Can you locate it?

2	4	6	2	4	6	1	6	4	2	5	4
4	4	3	5	6	5	3	5	6	3	3	5
6	5	6	6	4	2	3	2	1	5	1	1
1	3	3	1	2	5	4	3	2	3	5	3
3	1	4	2	4	6	3	1	5	6	3	6
2	6	2	6	4	2	6	4	2	5	6	4
3	4	4	1	2	4	5	1	1	6	4	2
1	2	6	4	4	1	3	6	2	4	2	4
6	4	5	2	6	3	4	4	5	2	3	6
4	6	1	4	1	2	2	2	6	4	2	1
2	3	2	6	2	3	1	6	4	2	4	2
5	6	1	2	4	6	1	3	2	5	2	5

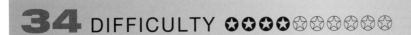 

34 DIFFICULTY ✪✪✪✪✪✰✰✰✰✰ | ④ Minutes

Make a calculation totaling the figure below by inserting the four mathematical operators (+, −, ÷, x) between the numbers shown.

They can be inserted in any order, and one of them has been used twice.

| 8 | | 4 | | 3 | | 5 | | 2 | | 6 | = | 3 |

35 DIFFICULTY ✪✪✪✪✪✪✪✰✰✰ | ⑥ Minutes

Here's a trickier one! Using the same principle as above try to complete the calculation. One of the mathematical operators has been used twice.

| 99 | 25 | 36 | 11 | 22 | 72 | = | 127 |

5 Minutes

Given that scales a and b balance perfectly, how many red balls are needed to balance scale c?

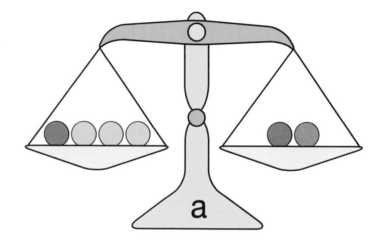

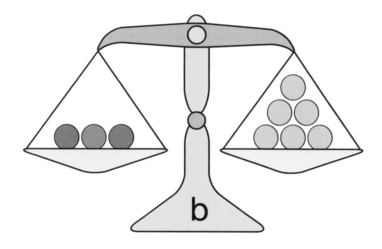

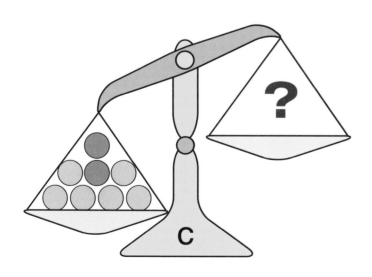

37 DIFFICULTY ●●●☆☆☆☆☆☆☆ ③ Minutes

The number 619362 appears just once in this grid and occurs in a straight line, running either backward or forward in a horizontal, vertical, or diagonal direction. Can you locate it?

1	3	9	1	4	2	6	4	9	1	2	4
2	2	6	3	6	9	3	2	6	4	6	3
6	4	6	9	2	1	2	1	9	3	6	2
3	6	2	4	3	6	9	3	1	2	9	6
9	2	9	1	9	3	4	4	9	6	3	3
1	2	1	6	6	1	3	2	6	3	6	6
2	9	6	3	1	9	6	3	9	2	2	1
6	1	2	3	6	4	9	6	1	3	1	9
3	9	3	1	9	3	6	2	2	6	6	6
9	4	2	9	2	1	3	1	9	2	1	2
1	2	1	3	1	3	6	4	3	1	4	1
4	6	9	1	3	2	6	3	1	9	6	9

38 DIFFICULTY ★★★★★★☆☆☆☆ ⏱ 7 Minutes

Place the remaining pieces in the grid so that:
* each row and column has two red and two yellow squares, and
* no row or column has two of the same digit.

2			4

| 4 | 3 |

| 5 | 2 |

2
4

1
4

5
3

1
3

| 5 | 1 |

39 DIFFICULTY ✪✪✪✪✪✩✩✩✩✩ ④ Minutes

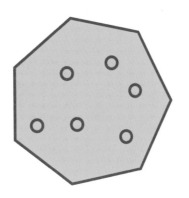

is to:

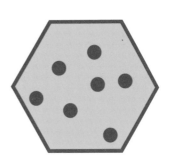

as

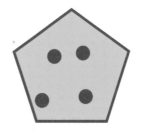

is to:

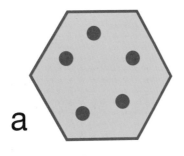

a

b

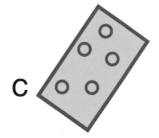

c

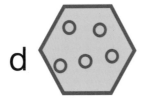

d

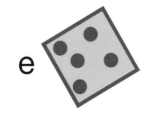

e

40 DIFFICULTY ✪✪✪✪✪✪✩✩✩✩ — ③⓪ Minutes

See if you can rise to the challenge and complete this numeropic. See the panel in puzzle 12 for instructions on how to complete this type of puzzle.

Top clues (by column):

```
                                        2
                            1   1       2   1
                    1       2   6 1     8 2   1
        2 4 5 6 8       10 9   2 7 8 5 6   6 5 1 6 3 5
        1 1 1 2 4 3 10 11 12 4 6 1 1 6 6 8 6 9 7 7 6 3 7 1 13     9 6 5 1
        2 2 4 2 4 2 4 3 3 1 1 7 11 2 6 1 10 7 1 1 5 1 4 6 6 11 7 6 3 1
        1 1 1 7 1 1 1 1 1 2 1 1 13 1 1 2 1 1 12 1 1 2 1 1 1 1 1 10 1 1 1 1
```

Left clues (by row):

```
                                  8
                                3 3
                                4 3
                          3 1 5 2
                              4 7 2
                              5 5 3
                              6 5 5
                              6 7 6
                  8 1 1 1 1 6
                              8 7
                            7 8 5
                            7 9 4
                            7 10 3
                            6 10 3
                            6 10 2
                        5 2 3 3 2
            1 1 4 2 1 1 1 2 2
              1 1 2 2 3 3 1 1
                    1 1 1 13 1
                        5 13 1
                          19 2
                          17 5
                          14 6
                        3 4 4 7
                        5 2 2 9
                        5 2 2 7
                        3 4 3 5
              1 1 1 1 1 1 1 1
                1 1 1 1 1 1 1
                          30
```

MINDW⚙RKS BRAIN TRAINING

41 DIFFICULTY ✪✪✪✪✪✩✩✩✩✩

5 Minutes

Each block is equal to the sum of the two numbers beneath it. Can you find all the missing numbers?

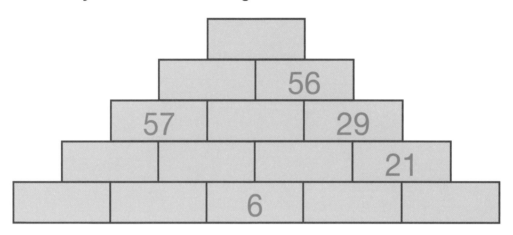

42 DIFFICULTY ✪✪✪✪✩✩✩✩✩✩

3 Minutes

Where should the hour hand point to on clock e?

The ace, 2, 3, and 4 in each of four suits should be placed in the grid below. Digits and letters showing the values A, 2, 3, and 4 and the suits have been shown at the beginning of each row across and column down to indicate which values and suits are contained in those rows and columns. Can you figure out the unique place for each card?

A A / 3 4	A 2 / 3 4	A 2 / 2 4	2 3 / 3 4
♥ ♥ / ♣ ♣	♥ ♦ / ♠ ♠	♥ ♣ / ♦ ♠	♣ ♦ / ♦ ♠

A A / 2 3	♥ ♣ / ♦ ♠			
2 3 / 3 4	♥ ♣ / ♦ ♠			
A A / 3 4	♦ ♦ / ♣ ♠			
2 2 / 4 4	♥ ♥ / ♣ ♠			

41

44 DIFFICULTY ✪✪✪✪✪✪✪☆☆☆ ⏱ 30 Minutes

You'll probably be over the moon when you've completed this numeropic. See the panel in puzzle 12 for instructions on how to complete this type of puzzle.

45 DIFFICULTY ✪✪✪✪✩✩✩✩✩✩  3 Minutes

The number 302949 appears just once in this grid and occurs in a straight line, running either backward or forward in a horizontal, vertical, or diagonal direction. Can you locate it?

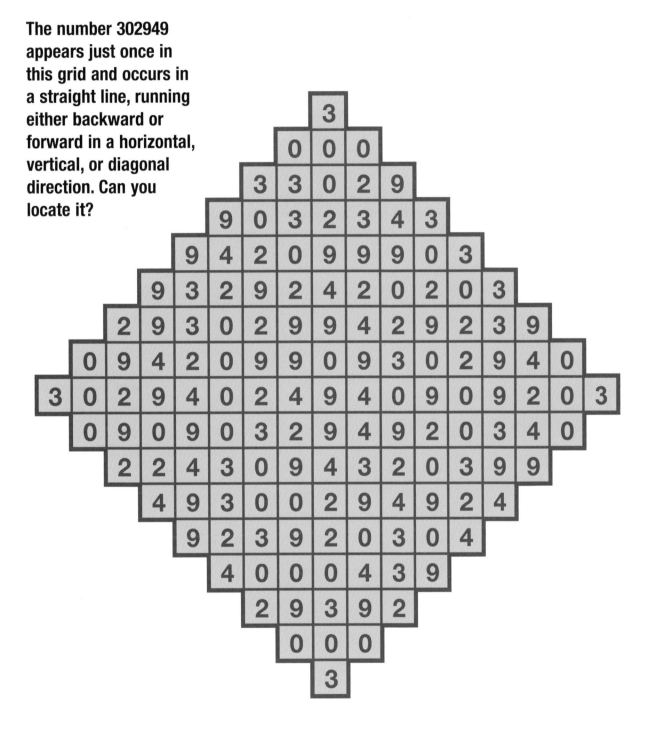

46 DIFFICULTY ✪✪✪✪✪✪☆☆☆☆ | ④ Minutes

What comes next in the above sequence?

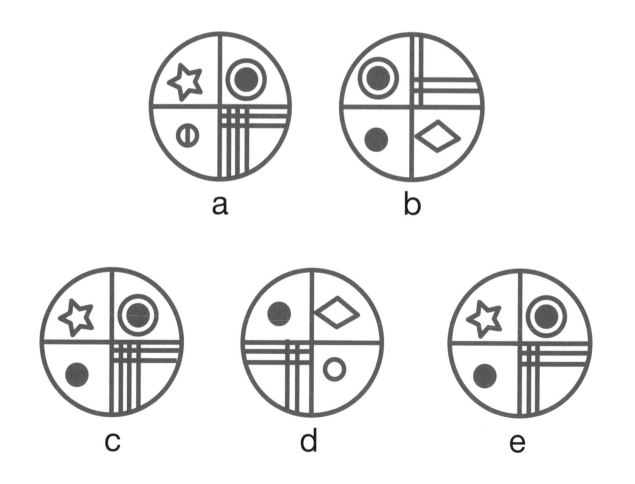

a   b

c   d   e

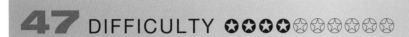

47 DIFFICULTY ✪✪✪✪☆☆☆☆☆☆  2 Minutes

Which is the odd one out?

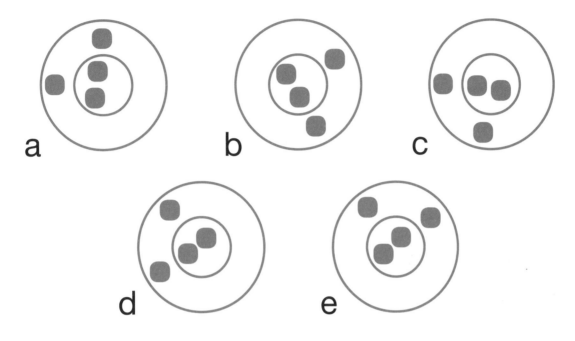

a   b   c

d   e

48 DIFFICULTY ✪✪✪✪✪✪☆☆☆☆  4 Minutes

On petri dish a there are currently 5,000 bacteria that produce another 250 bacteria per hour. On petri dish b there are currently 12,000 bacteria, but 100 bacteria die per hour. When will both dishes have an identical bacteria population?

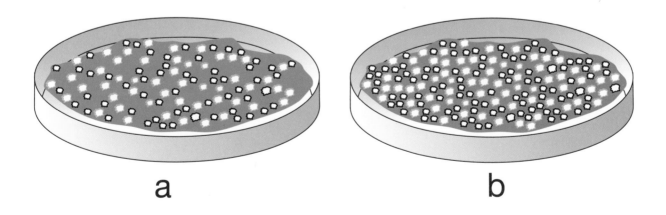

a   b

49 DIFFICULTY ✪✪✪✪✪✩✩✩✩✩   ⑤ Minutes

Can you fit these numbers into the grid? One number has already been inserted to help you get started.

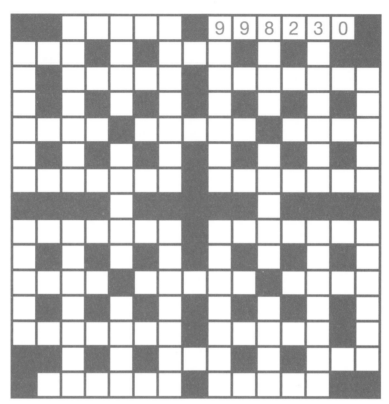

3 DIGITS
376
579
798
964

4 DIGITS
1560
2258
3065
4696
5862
7213
8024
9332

5 DIGITS
17686
21019
33644
46399
59575
66796
74716
84664
94955
99145

6 DIGITS
546262
695591
782758
998230

7 DIGITS
1266562
1745427
2137924
2735436
3675684
4487579
5997674
6337004
6727751
7178438
7912329
8148431
9467952
9945593

50 DIFFICULTY ✪✪✪✪✪✪✪☆☆☆ ⏱ (7) Minutes

Can you crack the safe? First decide which of the 14 statements given are false, then shade out the areas on the combination lock that are labeled with the letters of those false statements (so if you think statement A is false, shade out area A). The remaining lit segments will give you the digital combination required.

Hint: four of the statements are false.

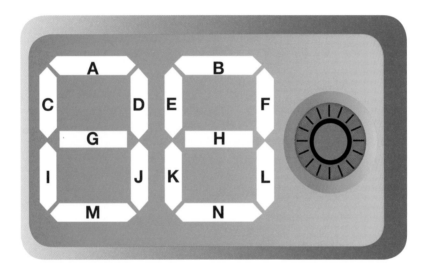

A. There are a dozen dozens in a gross.
B. 39 is a prime number.
C. 111 x 111 = 12,321.
D. 50 divided by 0.5 equals 25.
E. The total score you get from rolling two standard dice is 7, on average.
F. The positive square root of 121 is 11.
G. (1/2) x (2/3) x (3/4) x (4/5) = 1/5.
H. There are 1,440 minutes in a typical day.
I. If the digits of a whole number add up to 9, the number is divisible by 9.
J. "Threescore years and ten" equals 70 years.
K. If P x Q = Q, then P must be 1.
L. If two angles in a triangle are 36 and 54 degrees, the third angle is a right angle.
M. In Roman numerals, I + V + X + L + C + D + M = 1,666.
N. The cube of 5 is 225.

51 DIFFICULTY ✪✪✪✪✪☆☆☆☆☆   8 Minutes

Five owners brought their dragsters to race. Can you match each racer with his last name, name the cars, and find out each car's speed?

1. **Steve's Blisterine wasn't the fastest, and neither was the dragster owned by Zak Dupris.**
2. **Van Happs's Hot Stuff was 25 mph slower than one car, but only 10 mph slower than Jackson.**
3. **Marty was second quickest—20 mph quicker than Chicken Speed.**
4. **Fast and Loose wasn't the quickest, but it was quicker than Bubba.**
5. **Schwartz was quicker than Delaney.**

	Jackson	Delaney	Schwartz	Dupris	Van Happs	235	240	250	255	265	Rock Racer	Blisterine	Hot Stuff	Chicken Speed	Fast and Loose
Steve															
Zak															
Bubba															
Marty															
Kate															
Rock Racer																
Blisterine																
Hot Stuff																
Chicken Speed																
Fast and Loose																
235																
240																
250																
255																
265																

52 DIFFICULTY ✪✪✪☆☆☆☆☆☆☆   4 Minutes

Make a calculation totaling the figure on the right by inserting the four mathematical operators (+, −, ÷, x) between the numbers shown.

The mathematical operators can be in any order, and one of them has been used twice.

| 4 | | 6 | | 5 | | 2 | | 7 | | 3 | = | 8 |

53 DIFFICULTY ✪✪✪✪✪✪✪☆☆

8 Minutes

Make your way from top left to bottom right in this number maze. You may only move to calculations that total either one more or one less than the previous sum.

$22 \div 11$	$24 \div 6$	$36 \div 6$	$63 \div 9$	$3 + 3$
$34 \div 34$	$11 - 8$	5×1	$2 + 1$	$4 + 4$
$11 - 9$	$20 \div 4$	$0 + 4$	$11 - 6$	$2 + 5$
3×1	$3 + 2$	$5 \div 1$	2×5	$24 \div 3$
$36 \div 9$	$21 - 8$	3×4	$13 - 4$	$22 - 13$
7×2	$25 \div 5$	$8 + 3$	$70 \div 10$	$18 \div 2$
$1 + 6$	3×5	$23 - 10$	$6 + 5$	$16 - 6$
$21 \div 3$	$21 - 7$	$2 + 11$	$39 \div 3$	$5 + 9$
4×2	3×3	2×5	6×2	5×3
$28 \div 4$	5×2	$5 + 8$	2×8	$27 - 12$

MINDWORKS BRAIN TRAINING

54 DIFFICULTY ✪✪✪✪✪✪☆☆☆✪   ⏱ 30 Minutes

Can you keep on the right track with this numeropic? Refer to the instructions on how to do this puzzle in puzzle 12 if you need any help.

Column clues (top):

													2		3														
1	1		2	2	2	1	4	2	3	6						3	
13	1	1	7	2	4	3	3	3	1	5	6	2	3	2	1	14	3	3	5	3
13	2	13	7	2	7	2	1	1	1	2	1	1	2	8	7	13	2	5	5	2	5	6
4	1	13	2	1	3	3	2	2	2	2	2	2	2	3	3	2	2	2	2	2	3	3	1	2	6	3	3	2
13	1	11	4	2	1	2	2	1	2	1	1	1	2	1	2	2	1	2	1	2	1	2	2	1	2	4	14	1	3
1	2	2	2	1	1	2	3	2	2	1	1	1	2	2	3	2	1	1	2	2	2	2	2	1	2	2	2	1	1

Row clues (left):

| 7 |
| 8 |
| 4 | 3 |
| 3 |
| 3 |
| 8 |
4	10
6	10
4	2	1
4	1	2	1
4	3	2	2
4	5	2	1
19	1
20	2
27
10	11
9	10
10	11
26
1	1
1	26	1
30
1	2	2	2	2	2	1
2	1	1	1	1	1	1	2
1	18	1
1	2	1	1	2	1	1	2	1
1	1	1	1	1	1	1
2	2	2
30
3	3	3	3	3

55 DIFFICULTY ✪✪✪✪✪✪☆☆☆☆ ⏱ 5 Minutes

The number 295617 appears just once in this grid and occurs in a straight line, running either backward or forward in a horizontal, vertical, or diagonal direction. Can you locate it?

```
        2 9 5
      6 1 7 2 9 5 6
    1 7 2 9 5 6 7 7 2
    9 5 6 1 7 2 6 7 5 9 1
  2 2 7 2 9 5 9 1 2 7 5 7 2
  7 9 9 9 6 2 5 2 6 9 6 6 1
9 2 5 6 1 7 2 6 1 2 5 1 9 5 2
2 5 9 6 1 9 5 5 6 9 2 9 5 1 9
2 9 5 1 5 6 9 7 7 5 6 7 2 6 5
  9 7 6 5 2 7 2 1 7 6 1 7 2
  7 9 1 2 6 1 1 6 1 5 6 9 5
    7 5 9 1 2 9 5 6 7 9 2
    2 6 7 6 5 9 9 1 9
      7 2 5 9 2 9 2
        9 2 5
```

56 DIFFICULTY ★★★★★★☆☆☆ — 7 Minutes

Each block is equal to the sum of the two numbers beneath it. Can you find all the missing numbers?

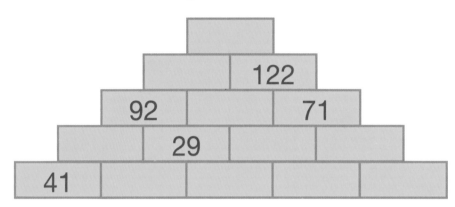

57 DIFFICULTY ★★★★★☆☆☆☆☆ — 8 Minutes

Five workers at a candy factory all have different jobs on different lines. Can you match each first name to a last name, a product, and a job?

	Toggle	Duffy	Button	Hopper	Dorrit	Packing	Quality control	Wrapping	Orders	Tasting	Fudge	Truffles	Mints	Caramels	Lollipops
Deborah															
Diane															
Brenda															
Bob															
Brian															
Fudge															
Truffles															
Mints															
Caramels															
Lollipops															
Packing															
Quality Control															
Wrapping															
Orders															
Tasting															

1. Mr. or Mrs. Dorrit works with fudge and not with Brenda.
2. Diane Toggle doesn't wrap and she doesn't work with mints or truffles.
3. Bob in orders doesn't deal with caramels.
4. No one with a first name that begins with "B" works in quality control.
5. There are no women in lollipops and no men in mints.
6. The truffle taster is a woman, but she isn't Deborah Duffy.
7. Bob doesn't work in lollipops.
8. Mr. or Mrs. Button works in packing. Caramels are not wrapped.

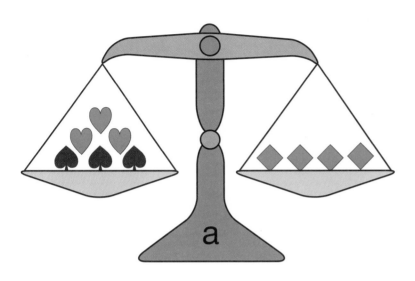

Given that scales a and b balance perfectly, how many hearts are needed to balance scale c?

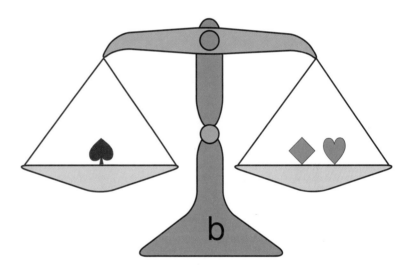

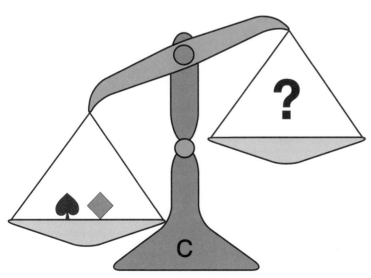

59 DIFFICULTY ★★★★★☆☆☆☆☆

5 Minutes

Each row and column contains the same numbers and signs, but they are arranged in a different order each time. Find the correct order to arrive at the final totals shown.

9	+	6	x	3	–	7	=	38
							=	28
							=	12
							=	33
=		=		=		=		
43		50		84		48		

 **1** Minute

We've given the cards shown here different values, so that an ace = 1, jack = 11, queen = 12, and king = 13, while all other cards have the same value as their numbers. Study this arrangement of cards carefully for one minute, then see if you can answer the questions on the next page.

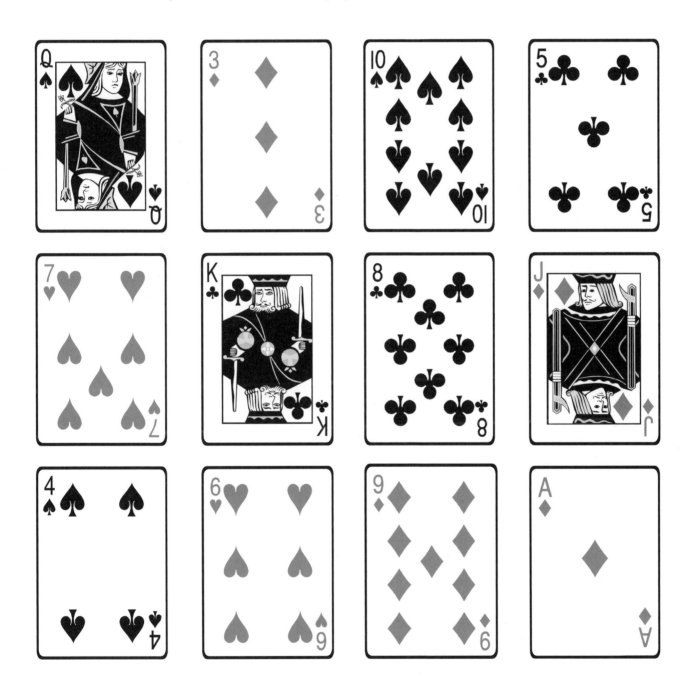

[60] DIFFICULTY ✪✪✪✪✪✪✪☆☆☆  **5** Minutes

Can you answer these questions about the puzzle on the previous page without looking back?

1. Which suit is the king?

2. Which number does not appear?

3. What is the lowest total value of four cards in a row?

4. What is the lowest total value of three cards in a column?

5. Which card is directly to the left of the 9 of diamonds?

6. What is the total value of the four corner cards?

7. Which suit is the ten?

8. Which card is directly above the 9 of diamonds?

61 DIFFICULTY ✪✪✪✪✪☆☆☆☆☆  **4** Minutes

Make a calculation totaling the figure on the right by inserting the four mathematical operators (+, −, ÷, x) between the numbers shown.

They can be inserted in any order, and one of them has been used twice.

10		7		11		4		8		12	=	19

Can you fit these numbers into the grid? One number has already been inserted to help you get started.

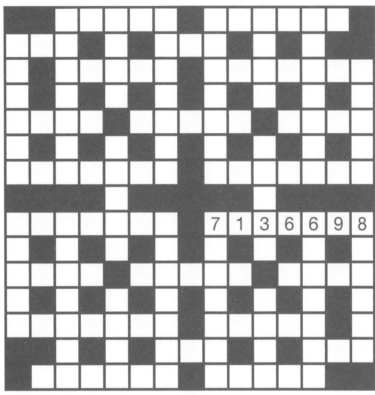

3 DIGITS
247
264
413
487

4 DIGITS
2528
3248
6283
6973
7184
8145
8831
9281

5 DIGITS
21643
28634
35138
38626
43196
54332
84461
86884
91798
95343

6 DIGITS
396889
442955
813158
895314

7 DIGITS
1582989
2413379
2757941
3396839
3397591
4845548
5558199
5597831
6317426
6489451
~~7136698~~
7641874
8744372
9159129

63 DIFFICULTY ✪✪✪✪☆☆☆☆☆☆  **3** Minutes

Take a close look at the patterned shields below. Which one is the odd one out?

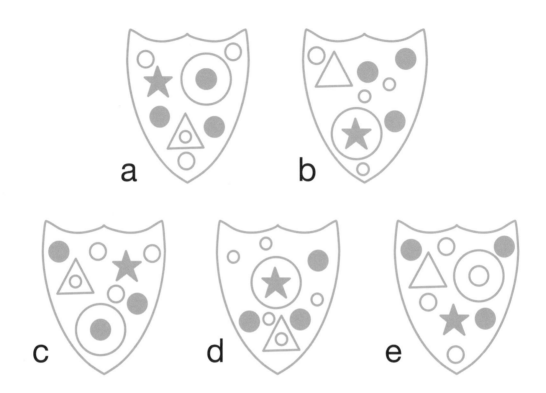

a b

c d e

64 DIFFICULTY ✪✪✪✪✪✪☆☆☆☆  **2** Minutes

What number comes next?

749326

239746

479236

??????

65 DIFFICULTY ✪✪✪✪✪✪✪✩✩✩  4 Minutes

The number 472596 appears just once in this grid and occurs in a straight line, running either backward or forward in a horizontal, vertical, or diagonal direction; however, as you can see, the numbers are reversed! Can you locate it?

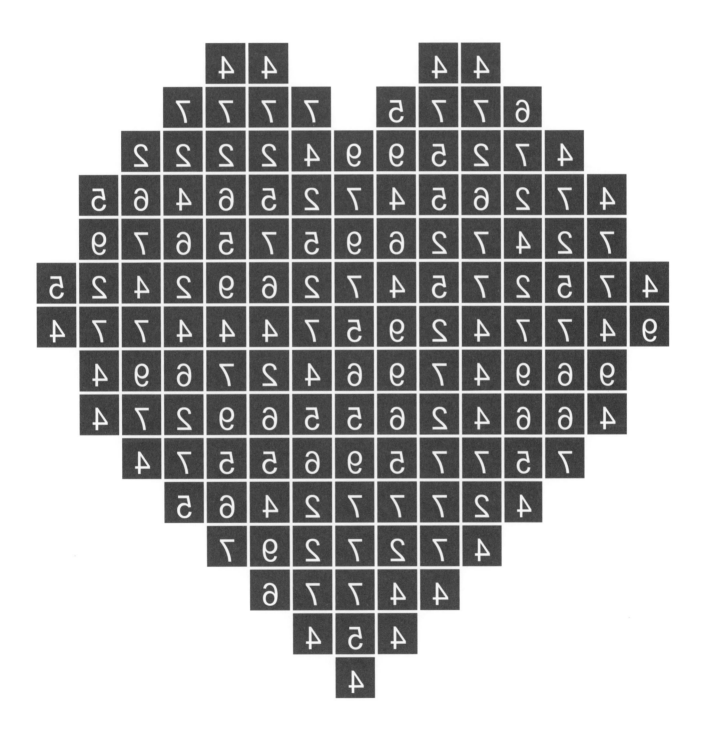

66 DIFFICULTY ✪✪✪✪✪☆☆☆☆

For this game, you will need three coins or counters for each player. The first player chooses a circle on the board to place the first piece. The second player then does the same. Play continues in the usual manner until all the players have played their pieces.

The aim is to get your three pieces in a horizontal, vertical, or diagonal line. If there is no winner after the first six opening moves, the first player chooses any coin and slides it along a line to any available adjacent circle. The second player takes a turn and so on. The first player to make a line of three wins the game.

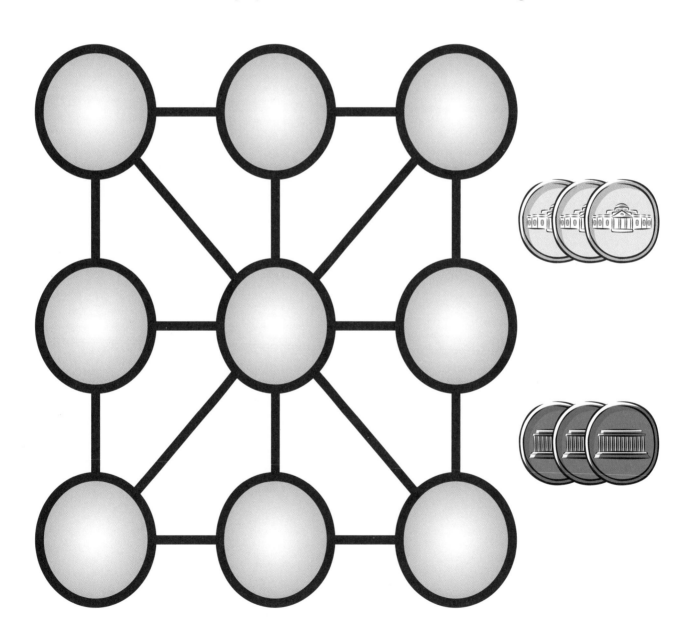

67 DIFFICULTY ★★★★★★☆☆☆☆

 30 Minutes

Can you steam through this numeropic in record time? If you need any help in completing this puzzle, refer to the instructions in puzzle 12.

Column clues (top):

```
                              1
                              2
                              1
                              1
                              1         1
                              1 1 1 1 3
                          1 1 2 2 2 2           1
    2 1 2 3 2     1 1 1 1 1 1 3 3 3 1 1 1 1 1   4 5 4 4 3 2
  1 5 6 7 8 9 2 21 1 1 1 1 1 21 21 21 21 21 21 21 21   4 4 4 4 4 4 14 12
  1 1 1 1 1 2 25 2 2 2 2 2 2 2 2 2 2 2 2 2 2 2 25 2 1 1 1 1 1 1 1 1
```

Row clues (left):

```
            4
            4
        4   6
        1   4
           14
  2 1 1    3
      2 16  5
  3 16 3    2
  7  9 3    2
      8 13  2
      6 12  2
      6 11  2
      6 11  2
      5  9  2
      4  9  2
      5  9  2
      3 13  3
      2  9  4
      3  9  4
      2  9  4
         2 14
         3 13
         2 12
         2 11
         3  9
         2  9
           16
        1   1
           16
           30
```

68 DIFFICULTY ✪✪✪✪✪✩✩✩✩✩

4 Minutes

Make a calculation totaling the figure on the right by inserting the four mathematical operators (+, −, ÷, x) between the numbers shown.

They can be inserted in any order, and one of them has been used twice.

| 20 | | 14 | | 9 | | 6 | | 18 | | 3 | = | 44 |

69 DIFFICULTY ✪✪✪✪✪✪✩✩✩✩

3 Minutes

Use your powers of logic to determine what number comes next in the sequence below.

36, 91, 21, 51, 82, 12, 42, ?

70 DIFFICULTY ✪✪✪✪✪✪✪☆☆☆  5 Minutes

Each block in this number pyramid is equal to the sum of the two numbers beneath it. Can you deduce all the missing numbers?

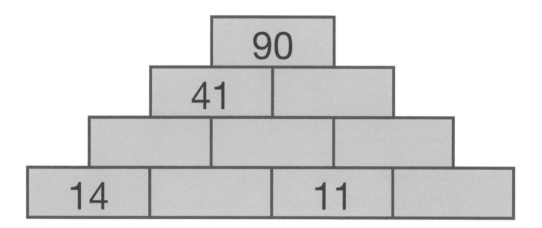

71 DIFFICULTY ✪✪✪✪✪✪☆☆☆☆  5 Minutes

If you saw these somewhat eccentric clocks on an office wall, what would be the logical time for GEORGETOWN?

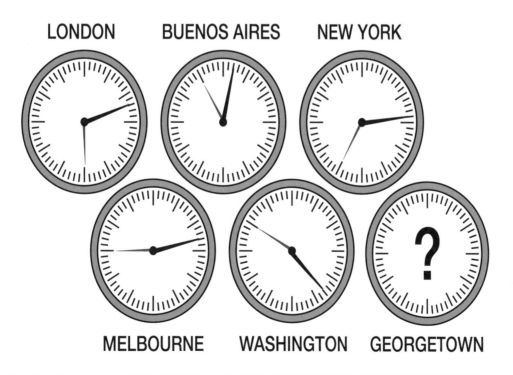

72 DIFFICULTY ★★★★★☆☆☆☆☆

5 Minutes

Which of the four boxed figures (a, b, c, or d) completes the set?

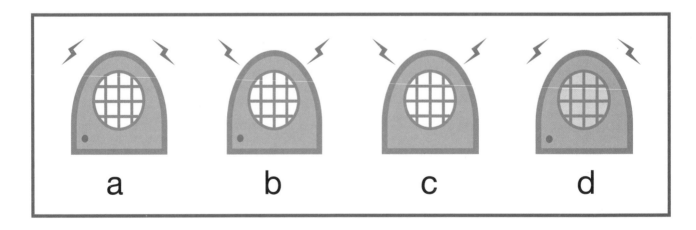

a   b   c   d

73 DIFFICULTY ✪✪✪✪✪✪✩✩✩✩ 7 Minutes

Place the loose tiles into the grid and ensure that:

* no row or column contains three tiles of the same color, and
* each row, column, and main diagonal adds up to 18.

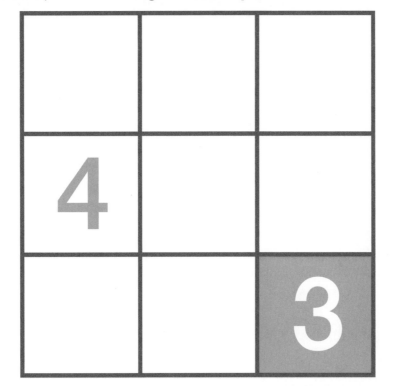

74 DIFFICULTY ✪✪✪✪✪✩✩✩✩✩ ⏰ 5 Minutes

Can you fit these numbers into the grid? One number has already been inserted to help you get started.

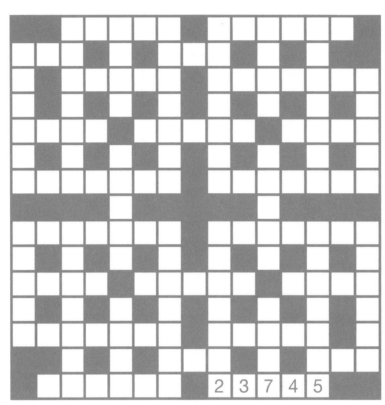

										2	3	7	4	5

3 DIGITS
197
318
795
816

4 DIGITS
1637
2596
3827
4622
5962
6241
8913
9677

5 DIGITS
12382
~~23745~~
39544
49833
54143
63416
77456
81758
82632
97188

6 DIGITS
151241
268298
663215
979198

7 DIGITS
1122752
1538888
2212918
3785942
3791668
4329272
5838986
5853511
6197375
7673189
8114462
8456616
9612239
9873892

75 DIFFICULTY ✪✪✪✪✪✪✪☆☆☆

1 Minute

Study these dice for one minute, then see if you can answer the questions on the next page.

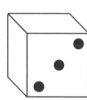
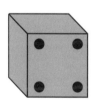
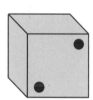

76 DIFFICULTY ✪✪✪✪✪✪✪☆☆☆

2 Minutes

A security guard is working a long night shift. At ten past one in the morning, he makes his first patrol. He patrols another four times at 70-minute intervals. He can then rest for a few hours before the patrol just after ten o'clock. He completes two more patrols with 70-minute gaps before clocking off at lunchtime. What superstition does he have?

[75] DIFFICULTY ✪✪✪✪✪✪✪☆☆☆   ③ Minutes

Can you answer these questions about the dice on the previous page without looking back?

1. What is the color of the die directly below the white die that has five spots?
2. What is the sum total of the number of spots on the two most central dice?
3. What is the color of the die directly to the left of the blue die with two spots?
4. What is the color of the die directly above the orange die with one spot?
5. What is the sum total of the number of spots on all of the pink dice?
6. What are the colors of the three dice that have only one spot?
7. Only two dice of the same color are horizontally adjacent to one another: what is the sum total of the number of spots on these two dice?
8. Only two dice are identical: what is the color of these two dice?

77 DIFFICULTY ✪✪✪✪✪✪☆☆☆☆   ③ Minutes

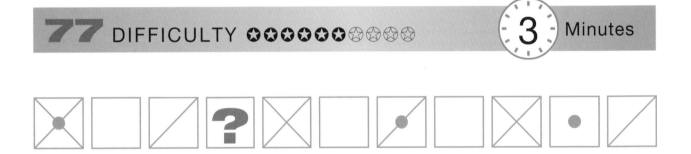

Which box below should replace the question mark in the above sequence?

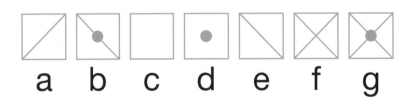

a   b   c   d   e   f   g

This puzzle uses the 16 face cards and aces from all four suits of a standard deck of cards. Complete the grid so that no row or column contains two cards of the same denomination or suit.

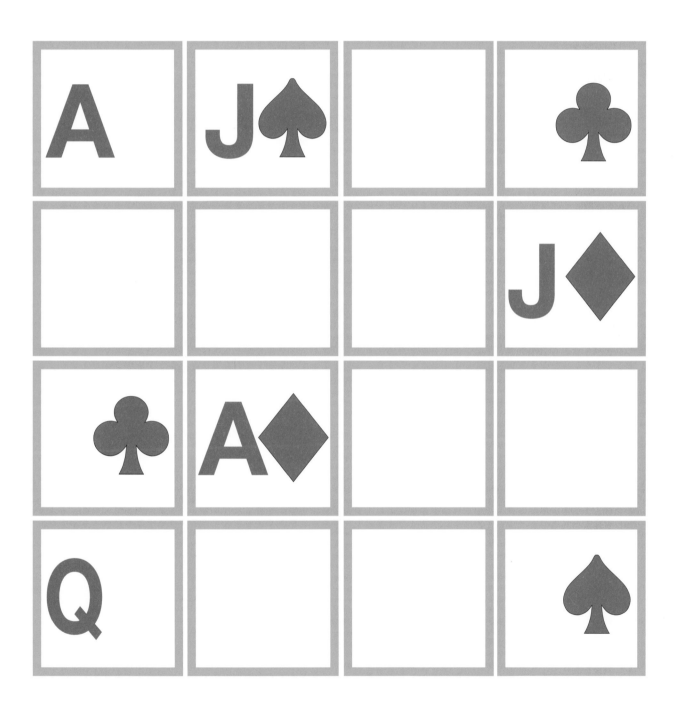

79 DIFFICULTY ✪✪✪✪✪✪☆☆☆☆  **6** Minutes

Can you crack the safe? First decide which of the 14 statements given are false. Then shade out the areas on the combination lock that are labeled with the letters of those false statements (so if you think statement A is false, shade out area A). The remaining lit segments will give you the digital combination required.

Hint: five of the statements are false.

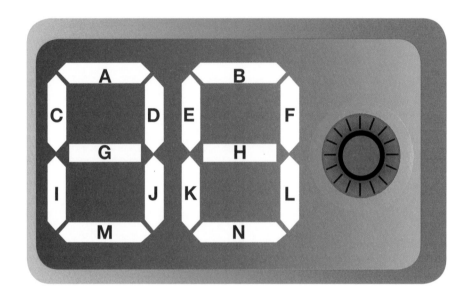

A. Ronald Reagan was the 40th president of the United States.
B. IQ stands for Intelligence Quota.
C. In architecture, a campanile is a bell tower.
D. In medieval times, a knight's glove was called a gauntlet.
E. The first Boeing 747 jumbo jet flew in February 1959.
F. A force 12 storm on the Beaufort scale is a hurricane.
G. Clint Eastwood won the Best Director Oscar for Unforgiven in 1992.
H. A lepidopterist collects coins.
I. Montezuma II was the last emperor of the Aztecs.
J. Limestone and chalk are forms of calcium carbonate.
K. Omega is the fourth letter of the Greek alphabet.
L. The real name of Batman is Bruce Wayne.
M. El Cid and Macbeth were born in the same century.
N. Cygnus cygnus is the Latin classification for the raven.

80 DIFFICULTY ★★★★★★☆☆☆☆ ④ Minutes

Complete the calculation totaling the figure on the right by inserting the four mathematical operators (+, −, ÷, x) between the numbers shown.

The mathematical operators can be in any order, and one of them has been used twice.

| 44 | | 11 | | 57 | | 39 | | 13 | | 86 | = | 200 |

81 DIFFICULTY ★★★★★★★☆☆☆ ⑥ Minutes

Take the cards around the outside of the grid and place them so that each horizontal row contains cards of six different values and each vertical column contains cards of four different values and four different suits. No card should be placed either horizontally or vertically next to one of the same color. The values of the cards are as per their numbers. Cards already in place should not be moved.

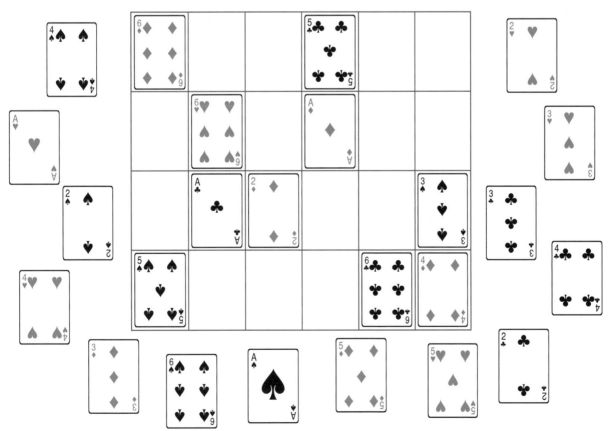

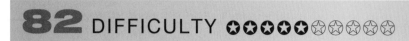

82 DIFFICULTY ✪✪✪✪✪✪☆☆☆☆☆  2 Minutes

Which number is the odd one out?

6839

7421

8243

2471

4283

3869

9263

83 DIFFICULTY ✪✪✪✪✪✪✪✪✪☆  5 Minutes

Each block in this especially difficult number pyramid is equal to the sum of the two numbers beneath it. Find the missing numbers.

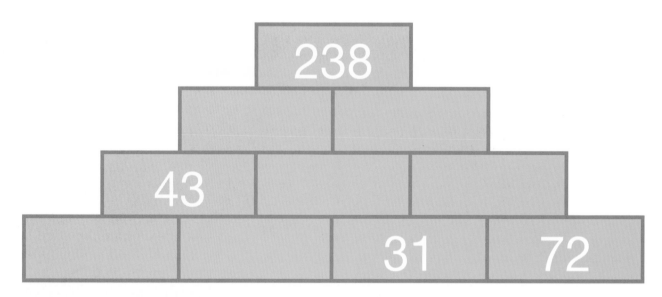

3682497

is to

9738642

and

285417

is to

751842

and

7186293

is to…

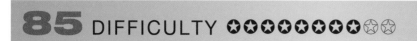

85 DIFFICULTY ✪✪✪✪✪✪✪✪☆☆  5 Minutes

Each of the blocks in this challenging number pyramid is equal to the sum of the two numbers beneath it. Can you find all of the missing numbers?

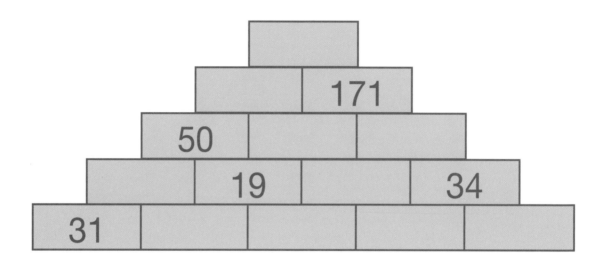

86 DIFFICULTY ✪✪✪✪✪☆☆☆☆☆ 4 Minutes

Make a calculation totaling the figure on the right by inserting the four mathematical operators (+, −, ÷, x) between the numbers shown.

They can be inserted in any order, and one of them has been used twice.

| 70 | | 86 | | 13 | | 66 | | 4 | | 27 | = | 171 |

Five soccer players, playing in different positions, scored a varying number of goals for their teams. Can you match each first name with a last name, a team, a position, and a number of goals scored?

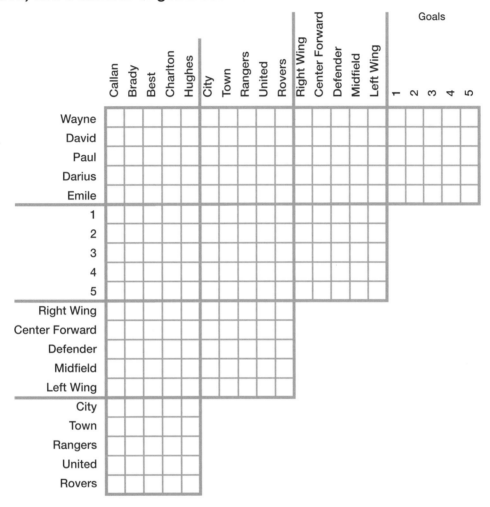

1. **Wayne Brady isn't a midfielder or a center forward. He scored more goals than Darius.**
2. **Rovers' Charlton scored more than Brady.**
3. **The Rangers' center forward scored two less than the Rovers' player.**
4. **Paul, playing for United, scored one more than David.**
5. **Hughes got four. He isn't a winger.**
6. **Emile, the left winger, scored two more than the center forward and one less than the Town player.**
7. **Callan got one less than the City defender.**

88 DIFFICULTY ✪✪✪✪✪✪✩✩✩✩

4 Minutes

Make a calculation totaling the figure on the right by inserting the four mathematical operators (+, −, ÷, x) between the numbers shown.

They can be inserted in any order, and one of them has been used twice.

| 14 | | 5 | | 33 | | 19 | | 4 | | 15 | = | 36 |

89 DIFFICULTY ✪✪✪✪✩✩✩✩✩✩

2 Minutes

Which number below is the odd one out?

3984 7456
1203 7896
5032 3527

90 DIFFICULTY ✪✪✪✪✪✪✪✪☆☆☆   ⏱ 5 Minutes

Given that scales a and b balance perfectly, how many spoons are needed to balance scale c?

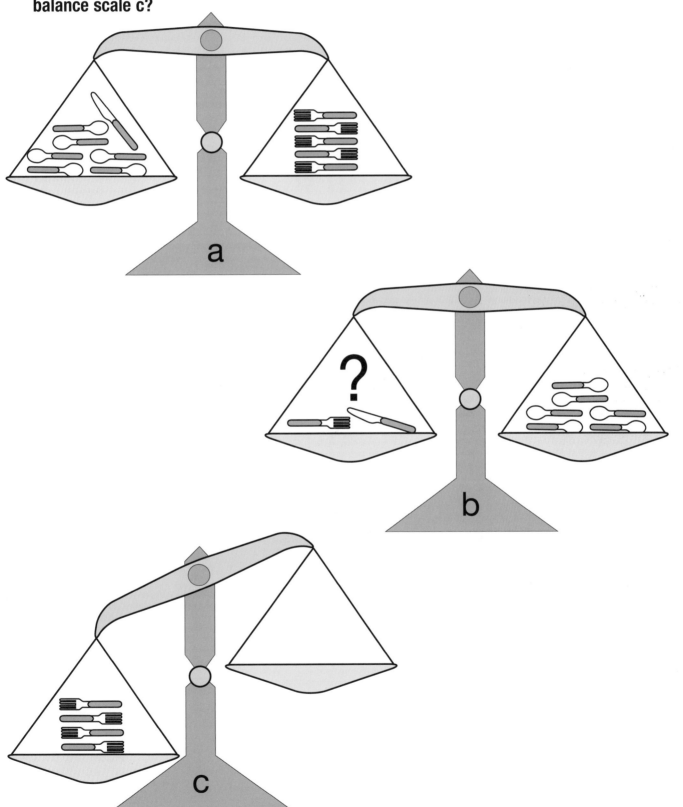

91 DIFFICULTY ✪✪✪✪✪✪✩✩✩✩ ⏱ 5 Minutes

This puzzle uses the 16 face cards and aces from all four suits from a standard deck of cards. Complete the grid by adding suits and face names so that no row, column, or main diagonal contains two cards of the same denomination or suit.

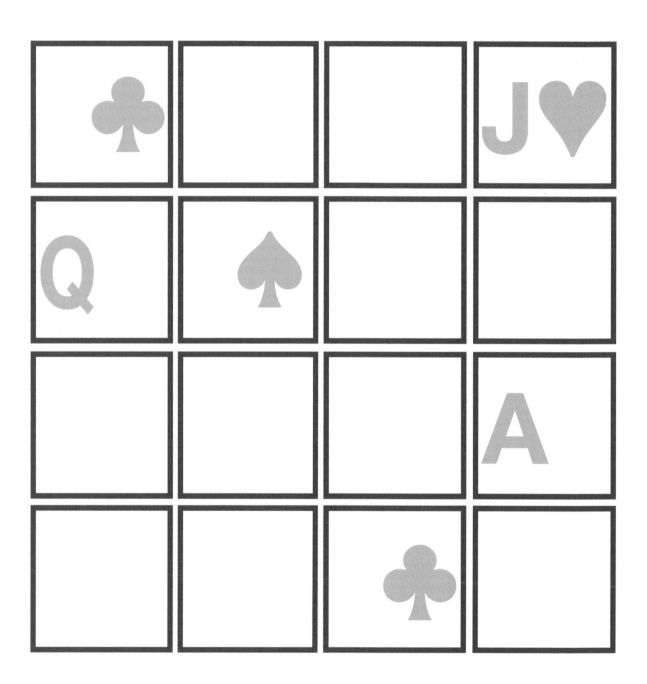

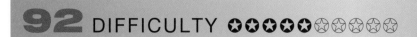

92 DIFFICULTY ●●●●○○○○○○ 4 Minutes

The following message has been encoded using a typewriter:

Yjr vpfr eptf od s voyu om Mre Uptl dysyr, ejovj od frdvtonrf sd s nodpm om yjr ID.

Look at the typewriter layout carefully and see if you can unscramble the sentence. Then figure out the seven-letter answer to the question it poses.

```
Q W E R T Y U I O P
 A S D F G H J K L
  Z X C V B N M
```

93 DIFFICULTY ●●●●○○○○○○ 2 Minutes

What number comes next?

3749216
629473
37496
?

94 DIFFICULTY ✪✪✪✪✪✪✪☆☆☆   ⏰ 3 Minutes

The numbers 2468 and 13579 each appear just once in this grid and occur in straight lines, running either backward or forward in a horizontal, vertical, or diagonal direction. Can you locate them both?

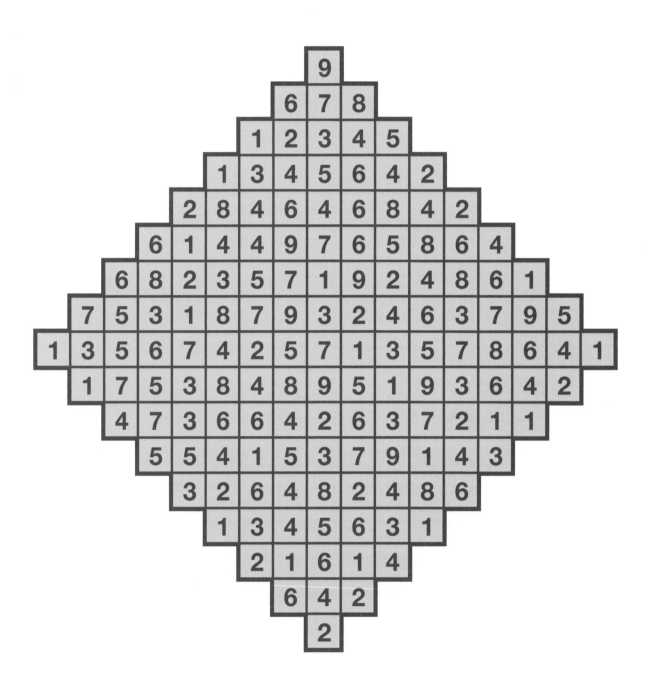

95 DIFFICULTY ★★★★★☆☆☆☆☆ 5 Minutes

Can you fit these numbers into the grid? One number has already been inserted to help you get started.

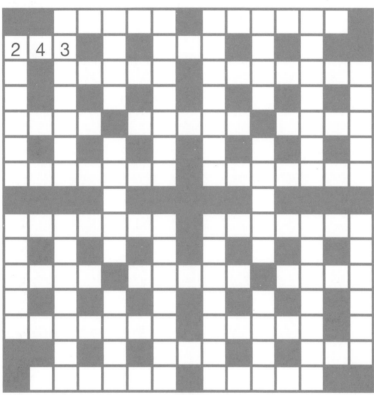

3 DIGITS
243
387
544
906

4 DIGITS
1855
3196
3327
4282
5178
7282
8924
9415

5 DIGITS
11547
23365
24444
32945
44795
52658
67358
71465
84394
92274

6 DIGITS
285743
444838
682584
735586

7 DIGITS
1344839
2688778
3496281
3667112
4311248
4778524
5611418
6589594
7359761
7585615
8148854
8824138
9299342
9569677

96 DIFFICULTY ✪✪✪✪✪✪✩✩✩✩ ③ Minutes

4837 is to **715**

and

6293 is to **155**

and

5978 is to **?**

97 DIFFICULTY ✪✪✪✪✪✪✩✩✩✩ ⑦ Minutes

Remove five cards from the grid and replace them in different positions so that the values of the cards in each row, column, and long diagonal line of cards totals exactly 25. The value of each card is as per its number.

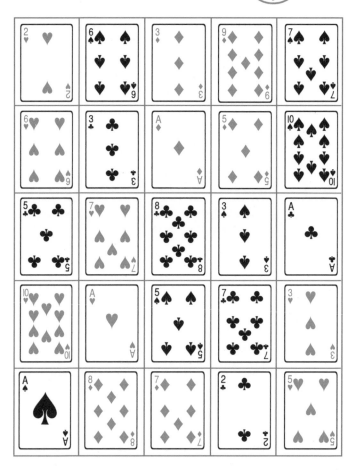

98 DIFFICULTY ✪✪✪✪✪✪✪✪☆☆ ⏰ 10 Minutes

Five children entered five different events at the school fair and finished in five different positions. Can you match each child to his or her last name, the event each entered, and the venue at which the event was held?

1. Bobby Macfie played marbles. There were only three competitors in the event and it wasn't on the soccer field.
2. The 3rd place finisher in the common room wasn't a girl.
3. The 4th place finisher in the hopscotch wasn't a girl or named Stuart.
4. The child who played Hacky Sack, not a Stuart, was placed higher than the child who jumped rope.
5. Wendy was in the playground. Young Macdonald and Macfie were not.
6. Betsy Campbell didn't win her event, which wasn't hopscotch, and wasn't held in the cafeteria.
7. Billy came first, but not in the Hacky Sack or marbles, and not on the soccer field.
8. The jump-rope event was held in the quad and was won by a girl.
9. The Hacky Sack competitor's first name didn't begin with "B" and he/she wasn't in the cafeteria or the common room.

	Campbell	Stuart	Macdonald	Lewis	Macfie	1st	2nd	3rd	4th	5th	Cafeteria	Playground	Soccer field	Common Room	Quad	Marbles	Hacky Sack	Hopscotch	Jump Rope	Jacks
Bobby																				
Billy																				
Wendy																				
Betsy																				
William																				
Marbles																				
Hacky Sack																				
Hopscotch																				
Jump Rope																				
Jacks																				
Cafeteria																					
Playground																					
Soccer field																					
Common Room																					
Quad																					
1st																					
2nd																					
3rd																					
4th																					
5th																					

99 DIFFICULTY ✪✪✪✪✪☆☆☆☆☆ ⏰ 5 Minutes

Make a calculation totaling the figure on the right by inserting the four mathematical operators (+, −, ÷, x) between the numbers shown.

They can be inserted in any order, and one of them has been used twice.

| 13 | | 27 | | 10 | | 15 | | 11 | | 9 | = | 72 |

100 DIFFICULTY ✪✪✪✪✪✪✩✩✩✩ ⏱ 6 Minutes

Each row and column contains exactly the same numbers and signs, but they are arranged in a different order each time. Find the correct order to arrive at the final totals shown.

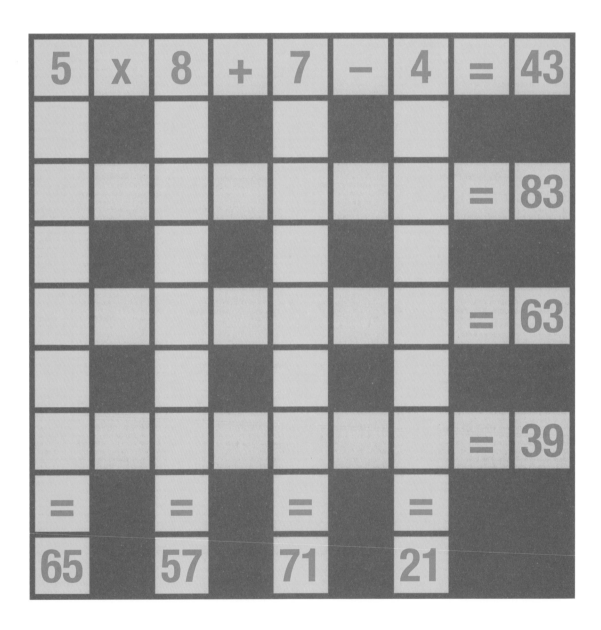

101 DIFFICULTY ✪✪✪✪✪✪✪☆☆☆

10 Minutes

There is only one logical way to get from a to b visiting all the patterns in this code maze. Can you find the hidden sequence by figuring out how the pattern changes from start to finish? Your lines may cross but you may not use any path or corner more than once.

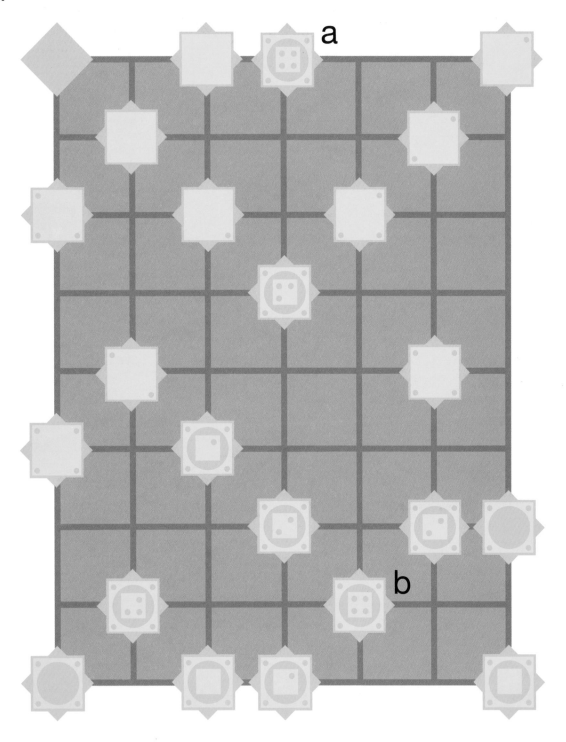

102 DIFFICULTY ✪✪✪✪✪☆☆☆☆☆

This is an interesting word variation of a popular logical game. It requires two players or teams, which we shall call the Setter and the Guesser. The Setter chooses a common five-letter English word that has all different letters. The Guesser then writes down his or her first guess as to what that word is.

The Setter helps the Guesser by drawing:
* a circle around correct letters that are in the correct place, and
* a square around correct letters that are in the wrong position.

In the example shown, the Guesser has taken five words to deduce the Setter's word. Players can now swap roles and see who can guess their opponent's word the quickest.

Beginners to this game might like to give their opponents the first letter of the word so that the opponents can begin their guesses with a purpose.

1. A S K E D
2. C H A S M
3. C I G A R
4. L O G I C
5. M A G I C

103 DIFFICULTY ✪✪✪✪✪✪✪☆☆☆

3 Minutes

Which of the boxed figures (a, b, c, or d) completes the set?

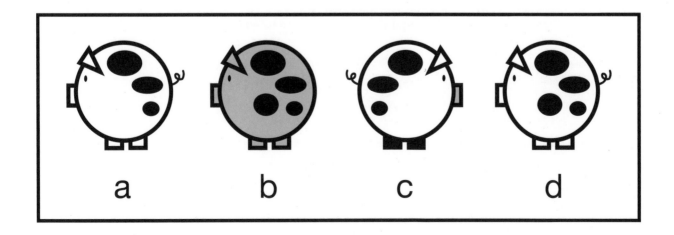

a   b   c   d

104 DIFFICULTY ✪✪✪✪✪✪✪☆☆☆ ③ Minutes

2634 7529 18

24 28

5816

Which two numbers, one in the group above and one in the group below, are the odd ones out?

42751698

20

16 23 9865

105 DIFFICULTY ✪✪✪✪✪✪✪☆☆☆ ③ Minutes

Two running partners follow the same route at the same time at the same pace. However, one measures his pace in terms of minutes taken for one mile, whereas the other uses kilometers per hour. Curiously, both statistics turn out to give the same number. How fast were they going? Assume 8 kilometers equals 5 miles.

106 DIFFICULTY ✪✪✪✪✪✪✪✪☆  7 Minutes

Each block in this difficult number pyramid is equal to the sum of the two numbers beneath it. Can you find all the missing numbers?

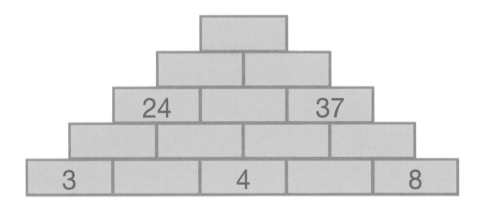

107 DIFFICULTY ✪✪✪✪☆☆☆☆☆ 3 Minutes

What numbers should replace the question marks in each line?

108 DIFFICULTY ✪✪✪✪✪✪✪✩✩✩   ⑤ Minutes

Can you fit these numbers into the grid? One number has already been inserted to help you get started.

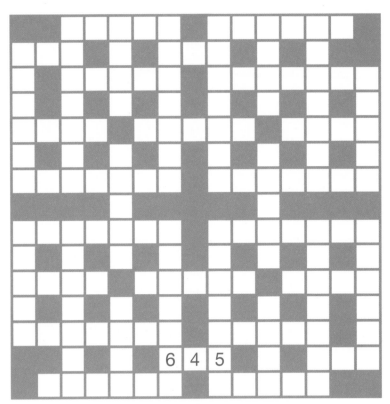

3 DIGITS	5 DIGITS	7 DIGITS
215	13124	1248958
261	14689	1638323
~~645~~	16877	2162177
728	22181	2173553
	24745	2374856
4 DIGITS	33621	3128791
1727	39713	3819862
2365	54366	4628248
4696	55923	5141821
5887	59228	6965163
6614		7429496
7521	**6 DIGITS**	8139288
9843	715785	8447319
9947	761584	9372633
	861383	
	861897	

109 DIFFICULTY ✪✪✪✪✪✪✪☆☆☆  30 Minutes

Blaze a trail to solve this numeropic. If you find it useful, refer to puzzle 12 for instructions on how to complete this puzzle.

Row clues (top to bottom):

			4	2
		4	2	2
	8	2	2	2
	1	2	5	2
			5	8
			4	6
		1	3	3
		3	7	3
5 1	4	1	3	
	2	4	8	3
9 1	4	1	2	
		10	5	4
	4	6	8	5
	2	8	9	2
		7	10	2
		7	11	2
		6	9	2
		7	8	1
			7	8
			6	8
			12	6
		6	4	6
	2	2	4	6
	1	2	4	5
	1	2	4	4
	2	1	2	4
	3	1	2	2
		2	2	1
			3	3
				30

110 DIFFICULTY ✪✪✪✪✪✪☆☆☆☆  4 Minutes

Can you place the tiles into the magic grid so that their numbers lie on the correct colored squares, and each row, column, and main diagonal adds up to 34?

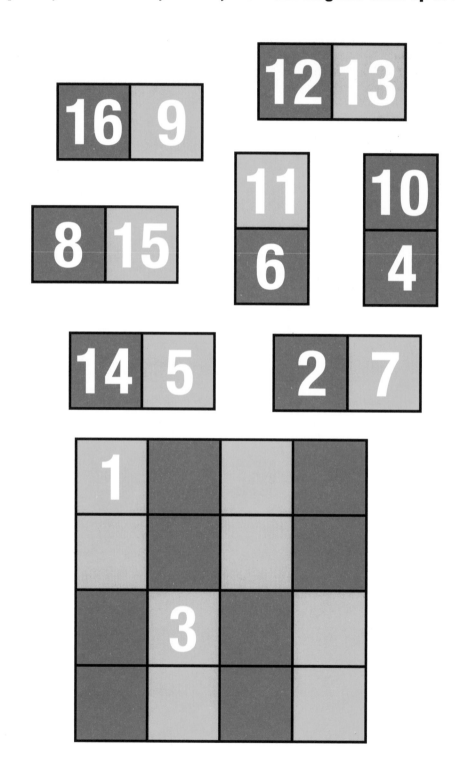

111 DIFFICULTY ✪✪✪✪✪✪✪☆☆☆ 5 Minutes

Each row and column contains the same numbers and signs, but they are arranged in a different order each time. Find the correct order to arrive at the final totals shown.

13	+	12	x	25	–	16	=	609
							=	121
							=	147
							=	336
=		=		=		=		
416		180		377		713		

112 DIFFICULTY ✪✪✪✪✪☆☆☆☆☆ ③ Minutes

Which pair of numbers is the odd one out? Why?

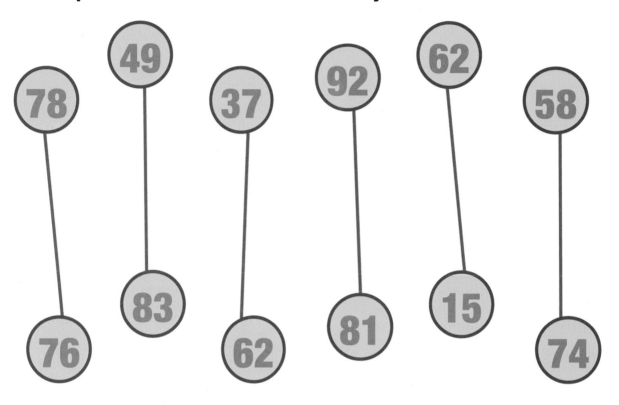

78 / 76

49 / 83

37 / 62

92 / 81

62 / 15

58 / 74

113 DIFFICULTY ✪✪✪✪✪✪☆☆☆☆ ② Minutes

An analog clock has fallen on the floor but is still operational. There is no way of seeing which way up the clock should go, but your perfect eyesight can tell that the minute and hour hands are pointing precisely toward two of the 60 tick marks on the clock face. Furthermore, the hands are exactly one tick apart.

So...what time is it?

114 DIFFICULTY ✪✪✪✪✪✪☆☆☆☆ 3 Minutes

7	9	3	6
5	8	7	2
8	4	3	6
5	8	2	9

is to:

4	9	4	6
9	5	9	8
3	2	6	2
8	7	3	7

as

7	2	6	4
3	8	9	7
6	5	8	3
5	4	5	6

is to:

3	6	3	5
4	5	8	2
3	8	7	8
8	3	5	6

a

4	7	3	6
6	9	8	5
2	8	5	4
7	3	6	5

b

4	7	2	6
5	4	9	3
4	9	8	7
7	2	6	5

c

8	3	7	3
4	7	8	6
7	4	9	2
4	5	4	5

d

115 DIFFICULTY ✪✪✪✪✪✪✪☆☆☆   ⏱ **6** Minutes

Can you crack the safe? First decide which of the 14 statements given are false, then shade out the areas on the combination lock that are labeled with the letters of those false statements (so if you think statement A is false, shade out area A). The remaining lit segments will give you the digital combination required.

Hint: six of the statements are false.

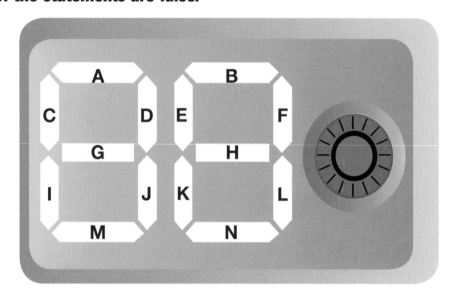

A. The elevator was invented by Otis in 1852.
B. The watt is a unit of power.
C. In heraldry, the color green is referred to as sable.
D. In the Nato phonetic alphabet, Q is for Quebec.
E. The 1988 Olympic Games were held in Los Angeles.
F. Stephane Grapelli was a famous jazz violinist.
G. Rosinante's horse was named Don Quixote.
H. The planet Pluto has one natural satellite called Charon.
I. Tia Maria is a liqueur flavored with oranges.
J. Pathophobia is a fear of diseases.
K. "As old as time itself" is an example of alliteration.
L. St. Boniface is the patron saint of Germany.
M. Coryza is the scientific name for German measles.
N. The United Nations was founded in 1945.

Each block is equal to the sum of the two numbers beneath it. Find all the missing numbers, then figure out the significance of the bottom row.

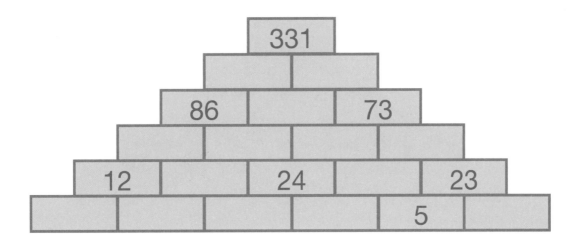

117 DIFFICULTY ✪✪✪✪✪✪☆☆☆☆  3 Minutes

What comes next?

4.5, 1.5, 4.5, 13.5, 10.5, 3.5, 6.5, ?

118 DIFFICULTY ⭐⭐⭐⭐⭐☆☆☆☆☆  ② Minutes

Which number is the odd one out?

8567   6589

4369   2189

8162   4328

119 DIFFICULTY ⭐⭐⭐⭐⭐☆☆☆☆☆  ② Minutes

What number comes next in the sequence?

100, 99.5,

98, 93.5, ?

120 DIFFICULTY ✪✪✪✪✪✪☆☆☆☆  1 Minute

We've given the cards below different values, so that an ace = 1, a jack = 11, a queen = 12, and a king = 13, while all other cards have the same value as their numbers. Study this arrangement of cards carefully for one minute, then see if you can answer the questions on the next page.

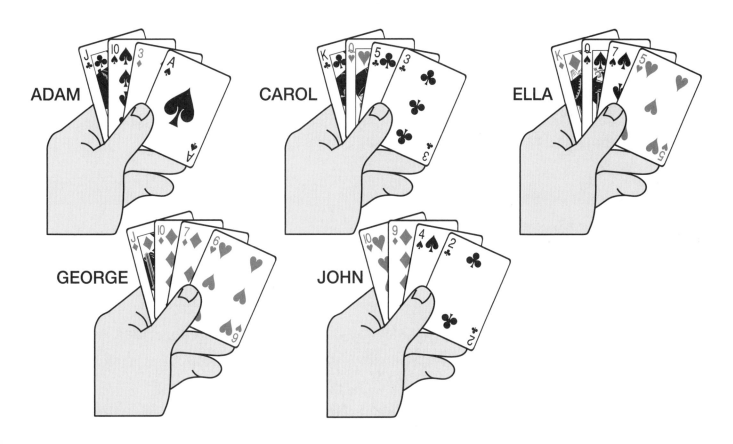

ADAM   CAROL   ELLA

GEORGE   JOHN

121 DIFFICULTY ✪✪✪✪✪✪✪✪☆☆  5 Minutes

Make a calculation totaling the figure on the right by inserting the four mathematical operators (+, −, ÷, x) between the numbers shown.

They can be inserted in any order, and one of them has been used twice.

| 25 | | 15 | | 87 | | 12 | | 79 | | 44 | = | 147 |

[120]   DIFFICULTY ✪✪✪✪✪✪☆☆☆☆   ① Minute

Can you answer these questions about the puzzle on the previous page without looking back?

1. Which player holds the queen of hearts?

2. Only one value of playing card is not represented in any of the five hands. Which one?

3. Which player has cards of the highest total value?

4. Two players hold cards with the same total value: which two players are they, and what is the value of the cards they hold?

5. What is the value of the club in John's hand?

6. Which player holds no black cards?

7. Which player holds the ten of hearts?

8. Only one player has an ace. Which suit is it?

122   DIFFICULTY ✪✪✪✪✪✪✪☆☆☆   ③ Minutes

Each block is equal to the sum of the two numbers beneath it. Can you find all the missing numbers?

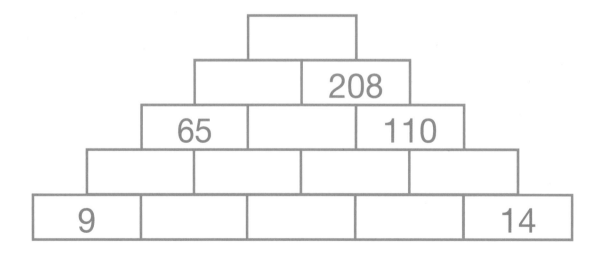

DEDUCTIVE PUZZLES

123 DIFFICULTY ●●●●●●○○○○  5 Minutes

Can you fit these numbers into the grid? One number has already been inserted to help you get started.

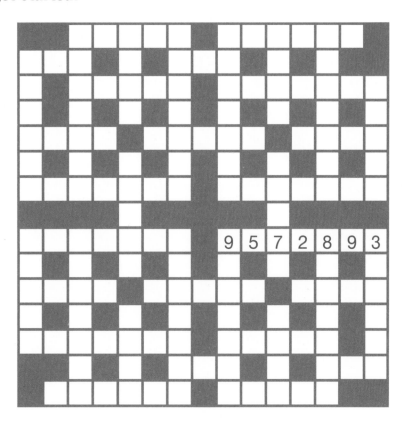

3 DIGITS
516
552
746
793

4 DIGITS
1424
2726
4649
6775
6958
7523
7957
8613

5 DIGITS
16466
24538
29534
31498
32179
58558
59383
68475
94741
96796

6 DIGITS
212589
353652
528888
712147

7 DIGITS
1956723
2675994
3945178
4281948
5346342
6585144
6636991
7421445
7811294
8263453
8541779
~~9572893~~
9625251
9745235

124 DIFFICULTY ✪✪✪✪✪✪✪☆☆☆   ⏱ (5) Minutes

Which of the four boxed figures (a, b, c, or d) completes the set?

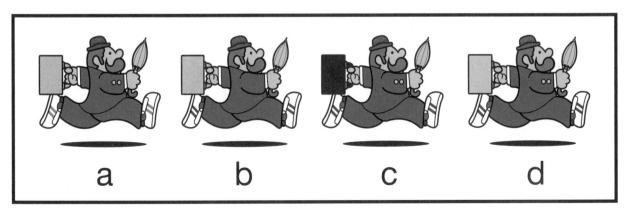

a   b   c   d

125 DIFFICULTY ★★★★★☆☆☆☆☆   8 Minutes

Solve the maze by filling the blank spaces with the four squares below so that the colors run from the top to the bottom in the correct order. The squares below may not be the right way up!

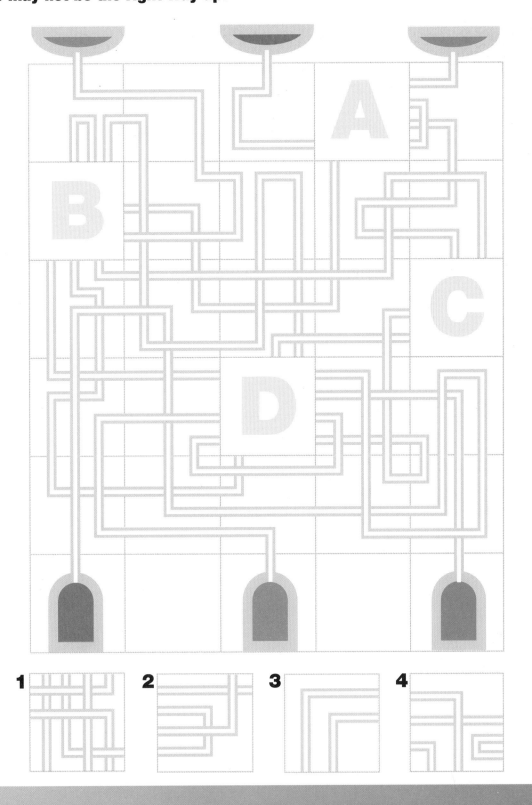

1 **2** **3** **4**

126 DIFFICULTY ★★★★★☆☆☆☆☆

Take a number of coins and place them in a circle with a different coin at the top. Two players take turns removing one, two, or three touching coins from the circle. The special coin must be taken last. The player who removes this coin at the very end of the game is the winner.

127 DIFFICULTY ★★★★☆☆☆☆☆☆  1 Minute

One hour ago, it was as long after 1 p.m. as it was before 1 a.m. What time is it now?

128 DIFFICULTY ★★★★★☆☆☆☆☆  3 Minutes

Which number is the odd one out?

a. 391221

b. 831114

c. 491322

d. 191029

e. 891726

f. 931215

MINDW RKS BRAIN TRAINING

129 DIFFICULTY ✪✪✪✪✪✪✪☆☆☆   ④ Minutes

Place the remaining tiles into the grid given that:
* there is one square of every color in every row and column, and
* each row, column, and main diagonal adds up to 34.

	14		**15**
16		**13**	

1	**2**	**3**	**4**
5	**6**	**7**	**8**
9	**10**	**11**	**12**

130 DIFFICULTY ✪✪✪✪✪✪✪✩✩✩   **5** Minutes

Write the numbers from 1 to 10 onto the bricks so that each block in the upper three rows contains the (positive) difference between the two numbers beneath it.

For example, if the top block was a 5, the blocks in the second row could be 7 and 2.

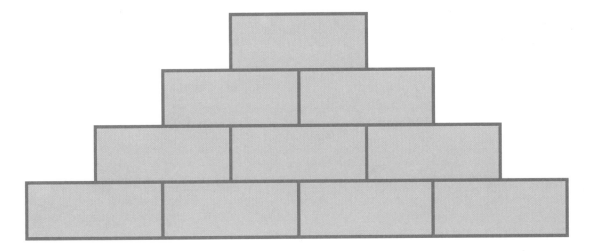

131 DIFFICULTY ✪✪✪✪✪✪✪✩✩✩   **3** Minutes

7296384 is to 3987462

as 6174258 is to 2756841

and 2917834 is to ?

ANSWERS

1

Square A is the correct move. It forces a win for Os. The other options will force a draw or possibly even a loss.

2

The combination is 29. Correct versions of false statements:

C. A league equals three nautical miles.

J. Hexadecimal is the number system for counting in groups of 16.

K. An obtuse angle has between 90 and 180 degrees.

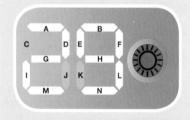

3

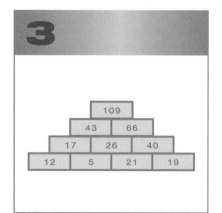

4

a; the dots change places in pairs working clockwise and starting with the top left/top middle dots.

5

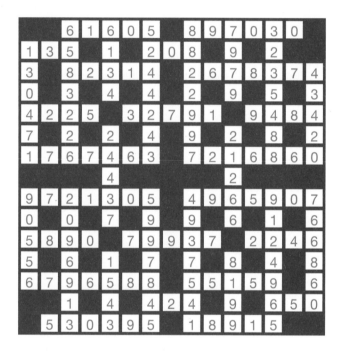

6

7

$2 \times 3 + 8 \div 7 \times 5 - 4 = 6$

8

Flo's animal is a chicken. The chicken was 2nd, so Flo was also 2nd (clue 1). Spot is a pig. Spot the pig didn't come 5th or 1st (2). Jack has a calf, and it placed 5th, so Jack placed 5th (3). Bob's animal is named Guffy, and it placed 4th, so Bob placed 4th (3). Norbert is a sheep, and his owner isn't Mavis or Flo (4), Guffy isn't a pig (2) or a sheep (4), and Bob doesn't have a calf (3) or a chicken (1). So Guffy must be a goat. Mavis doesn't own the chicken (1), the calf (3), or the sheep (4), and Bob owns the goat, so Mavis must own the pig, leaving Ned with Norbert the sheep. Mavis and Spot didn't come 5th or 1st (2), or 2nd (1), or 4th (3), so they came 3rd, leaving Ned and Norbert the sheep 1st. Guffy was 4th (3), and Tizzy placed higher than Pong (5), so Tizzy was 2nd and a chicken (1) and Pong was 5th and a calf (3).

Norbert—sheep—1st—Ned
Tizzy—chicken—2nd—Flo
Spot—pig—3rd—Mavis
Guffy—goat—4th—Bob
Pong—calf—5th—Jack

9

1. 4
2. 4+15+19=38
3. 4x19=76
4. Triangle (4) and cross (38)
5. 72
6. 7
7. The orange triangle and the orange cross
8. 89

10

Ten past one. Between any two clocks, 25, then 35, 45, 55, etc. minutes are added.

11

Nobel Peace Prize

12

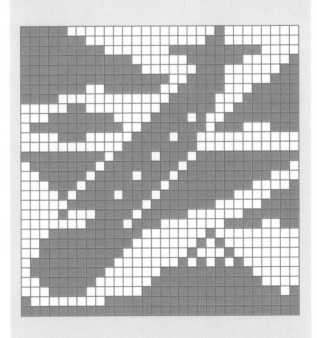

13

c; the figure retains the same shape, however, small circles change to large circles and vice versa.

14

They start and end with the same letter:

9:57   Nine fifty-seveN
8:23   Eight twenty-threE
1:32   One thirty-twO
11:25   Eleven twenty-fivE
9:13   Nine thirteeN
2:48   Two forty-eighT

15

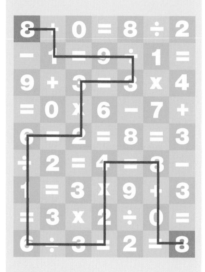

16

d; each vertical and horizontal line contains two dark-skinned and one light-skinned face. Each line contains a

face with one freckle, a face with two freckles, and a face with three freckles. Each line contains two eyes with two round highlights and one with a single round highlight. Finally, each line contains a blue eye, a brown eye, and a green eye. The missing image should be dark skinned with one freckle and a blue eye with two round highlights.

17

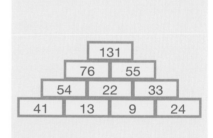

18

19

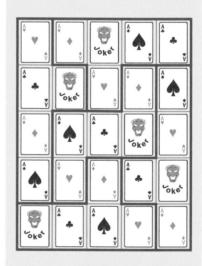

20

21

9 − 3 + 6 ÷ 2 − 4 × 5 = 10

22

10; one square and one circle weigh as much as five triangles. Thus one square weighs as much as three triangles, so a circle weighs as much as two triangles. Therefore, ten circles are needed to balance scale c.

23

d; a is the same string of dots as e, and b is the same string as c.

24

b; each vertical and horizontal line contains one red spade and two black ones. Each line also contains one image where the heart and club have been reversed and one image where the diamond has been turned on its side. The missing image should have a red spade, the club and heart should be reversed, and the diamond should be the right way up.

25

```
    1 3 1 5 2     4 4 2 2 8 2
6 9 3   9     2 2 6     4     2
1   6 0 9 8 3     5 8 7 1 1 6 4
6   5   3   9     3     6   8   2
9 3 7 9     2 7 8 5 6     4 3 6 8
3   0   5     5     0     1   6   4
7 6 3 8 6 6 3     4 7 2 0 9 5 2
        9                 9
3 3 6 8 2 8 7     9 4 6 5 2 6 8
5   9   2   7     2     8   8   8
3 4 6 5     9 1 3 0 9     7 4 5 6
6   0   5   0     2     6   5   0
5 5 2 1 6 6 1     8 9 1 1 6     3
      4   7   1 3 9     0     8 0 9
    3 2 0 7 3 0     7 2 7 7 6
```

26

The gold item Dupris wore was not Tom Buick (8), Canale (8), Fundi, or Armande (7), so it must have been Vergucci and a bag (4). The black item was not then Vergucci, or Tom Buick (9), Canale (6), or Armande, so it must have been Fundi. The pink hat wasn't Tom Buick or Fundi (2), Vergucci (4), nor Armande (5), so it must have been Canale. The red item must then have been Armande and Manon's. The pink hat wasn't Jody's (6), Kate's (2), Naomi Taylor's (8), or Manon's (5), so it must have been Emma's and she must be Emma Briant (8). Naomi Taylor wasn't then wearing a hat, gloves, or shoes (3), or the bag (belonging to Dupris)—she must have been wearing the coat. Naomi Taylor's coat must have been blue, as it wasn't pink (2), gold (7), black (6), or red (Manon). So Naomi was also wearing Tom Buick (9) and the gold bag was Kate's, making her Kate Dupris (7). The gloves weren't then blue, pink (2), red (5), gold (bag), or blue (coat), so they must have been black and Fundi and belong to Jody (6), and the shoes must be red and Armande and belong to Manon.

Ms. Jones didn't wear gloves (1), so the red shoes are hers, making her Manon and leaving the Fundi gloves to Ms. Heaton, who must then be Jodie.

Jody Heaton—Fundi—gloves—black
Kate Dupris—Vergucci—bag—gold
Naomi Taylor—Tom Buick—coat—blue
Emma Briant—Fundi—bag—pink
Manon Jones—Armande—shoes—red

27

b; the circle moves one corner clockwise, then two corners, then three corners, etc., at each stage and the line moves one corner only counterclockwise at each stage.

28

To win the game, play first and take two coins. Whatever your opponent does, leave 1, 8, or 9 coins (if you have taken an odd number of coins), or 4, 5, or 12 coins (if you have an even number of coins).

29

8; three cherries and one gooseberry balance one banana, thus four gooseberries plus three cherries weigh as much as eleven cherries, and four gooseberries weigh as much as eight cherries. So two cherries weigh as

much as one gooseberry. This gives the equivalent of two-and-a-half gooseberries in scale a balancing one banana, so five gooseberries weigh as much as two bananas. There are two bananas (equal to five gooseberries) and six cherries (equal to three gooseberries) in scale c. Thus eight gooseberries are needed to balance scale c.

30

107; add the digits of the previous number each time, i.e., 49 (+ 4 + 9) = 62, 62 (+ 6 + 2) = 70, 70 (+ 7 + 0) = 77, etc. Therefore 103 (+ 1 + 0 + 3) = 107.

31

5149; in all the others, add the first and third digits to produce the second and fourth digits, for example, 7141, where 7 + 4 = 11.

32

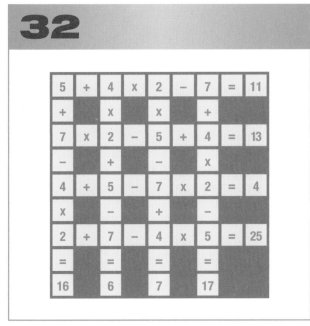

5	+	4	x	2	–	7	=	11
+		x		x		+		
7	x	2	–	5	+	4	=	13
–		+		–		x		
4	+	5	–	7	x	2	=	4
x		–		+		–		
2	+	7	–	4	x	5	=	25
=		=		=		=		
16		6		7		17		

33

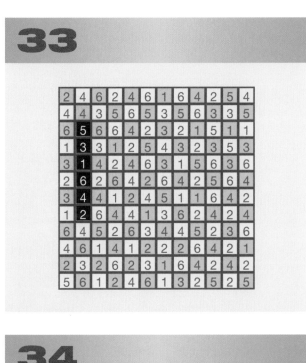

34

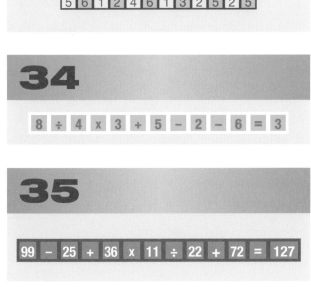

8 ÷ 4 x 3 + 5 – 2 – 6 = 3

35

99 – 25 + 36 x 11 ÷ 22 + 72 = 127

36

8; one blue ball weighs as much as three yellow balls, so two red balls also weigh as much as three yellow balls, and two red balls weigh as much as one blue ball. Thus eight red balls are needed to balance scale c.

37

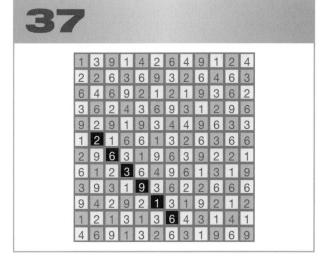

38

39

c; the large 5-sided figure (pentagon) reduces its number of sides by one and becomes a rectangle. The number of dots that are contained in the figure increase by one and change from black to white.

40

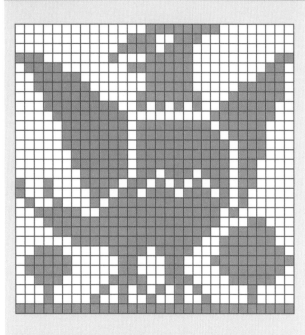

43

41

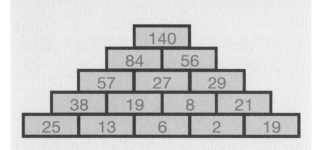

42

The hour hand should point to 7 o'clock. In the series, the minute hand is 30, 60, 90, 120, and 150 degrees clockwise from the hour hand.

44

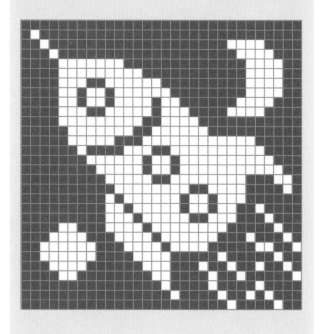

45

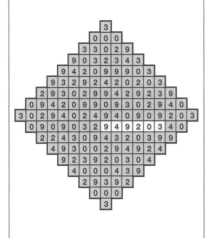

46

e; looking across the line of circles, the top left quarter alternates star/diamond, the top right quarter alternates circle with dot/circle, the bottom left quarter alternates white dot/black dot/dot with line, and the bottom right quarter alternates one line/two lines/three lines horizontally, and three lines/two lines/one line vertically.

47

d; all the others are the same figure rotated.

48

$5000 + 250x = 12000 - 100x$. Hence, $350x = 7000$, so $x = 20$. The numbers will be identical in 20 hours.

49

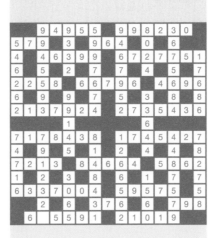

50

The combination is 64. Correct versions of false statements:

B. 39 is not a prime number because it is divisible by 13.
D. 50 divided by 0.5 equals 100.
K. If P x Q = Q, then P must be 1 as long as Q doesn't equal zero.
N. The cube of 5 is 125.

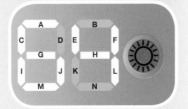

51

Blisterine is Steve's and didn't go 265 mph (1). Zak's last name is Dupris and he didn't go 265 either (1). Van Happs's car is Hot Stuff and it went 240 mph, and Jackson's went 250 mph (2). Marty went 255 mph and Chicken Speed went 235 mph. (3). Neither Blisterine (1), Hot Stuff (2), Chicken Speed (3), nor Fast and Loose (4) went 265 mph, so it must have been Rock Racer. Blisterine didn't go 265, 255, 240, or 235 mph, so it must have gone 250. Schwartz was faster than Delaney (5), so given that neither Dupris (1), Van Happs (2), or Jackson (2) went 265 mph, Schwartz must have. Zak Dupris didn't go 255 mph (3), so he must have gone 235, making his car Chicken Speed and leaving Delaney at 255, making his car Fast and Loose—and Delaney must be

Marty. Both Zak Dupris and Chicken Speed went 235 mph so that must be his car. Blisterine's owner is Steve (1), and Jackson's car and Blisterine both went 250 mph, so Steve is Steve Jackson. Fast and Loose was quicker than Bubba (4), so Bubba must have gone 240 mph, making him Bubba Van Happs, owner of Hot Stuff.

Steve Jackson—250 mph—Blisterine
Zak Dupris—235 mph—Chicken Speed
Bubba Van Happs—240 mph—Hot Stuff
Marty Delaney—255 mph—Fast and Loose
Kate Schwartz—265 mph—Rock Racer.

54

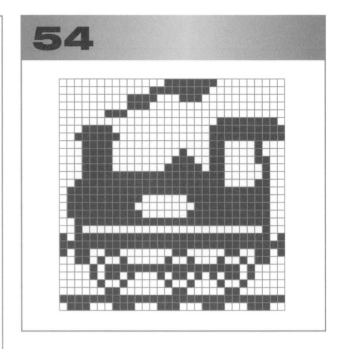

52

$$4 + 6 \div 5 \times 2 + 7 - 3 = 8$$

53

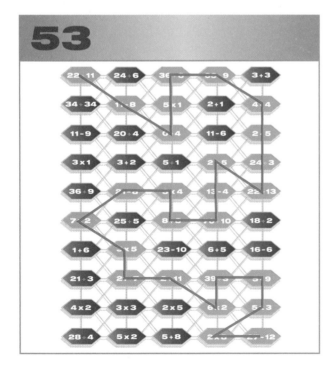

55

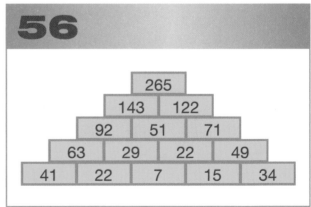

Number grid (puzzle 55):

```
            2 9 5
        6 1 7 2 9 5 6
      1 7 2 9 5 6 7 7 2
    9 5 6 1 7 2 6 7 5 9 1
  2 2 7 2 9 5 9 1 2 7 5 7 2
  7 9 9 9 6 2 5 2 6 9 6 6 1
9 2 5 6 1 7 2 6 1 2 5 1 9 5 2
2 5 9 6 1 9 5 5 6 9 2 9 5 1 9
2 9 5 1 5 6 9 7 7 5 6 7 2 6 5
  9 7 6 5 2 7 2 1 7 6 1 7 2
  7 9 1 2 6 1 1 6 1 5 6 9 5
  7 5 9 1 2 9 5 6 7 9 2
    2 6 7 6 5 9 9 1 9
      7 2 5 9 2 9 2
          9 2 5
```

56

			265			
		143		122		
	92		51		71	
63		29		22		49
41	22		7		15	34

57

Dorrit works in fudge, Brenda doesn't and she isn't Dorrit (1). Diane is Diane Toggle and she doesn't work in wrapping, mints, truffles (2), or fudge (1). Bob works in orders, not with caramels (3). Neither Bob, Brian, nor Brenda work in quality control (4). Deborah, Diane Toggle, and Brenda don't work in lollipops, and Bob and Brian don't work in mints (5). Deborah is Deborah Duffy (6). The taster works in truffles and is not Deborah, Brian, or Bob (6). Bob doesn't work in lollipops (7), caramels (3), mints (5), or truffles (6), so he must work in fudge and fudge must be in orders (3). Neither Deborah Duffy, Diane Toggle, Brenda, nor Bob work in lollipops, so that must be Brian. Button works in packing (8). Caramels are not in wrapping (8). Dorrit isn't Brenda (1), Diane (2), nor Deborah (6), and Brian doesn't work in fudge (1) so Dorrit must be Bob and Dorrit must work in fudge and orders. The truffle worker is neither Diane Toggle (2), Dorrit (1), Deborah Duffy (6), nor Button (8), so it must be Hopper. Hopper then doesn't work with lollipops, and neither do Toggle (5), Duffy (5), nor Bob Dorrit (7), so the lollipop worker must be Button. So Button doesn't work in mints and neither does Bob Dorrit (5), Hopper the truffle taster nor Diane Toggle (2), so Deborah Duffy is the mint worker, leaving Diane Toggle to work in caramels. Diane Toggle doesn't work in wrapping (2), packing (8), or orders (3), and truffles are in tasting so Diane Toggle works in the quality control department, leaving wrapping to Deborah Duffy.

Deborah Duffy—wrapping—mints
Diane Toggle—quality control—caramels
Brenda Hopper—tasting—truffles
Bob Dorrit—orders—fudge
Brian Button—packing—lollipops

58

13; one spade weighs as much as one heart plus one diamond; thus three spades weigh as much as three hearts and three diamonds. So one diamond weighs as much as six hearts and one spade weighs as much as seven hearts. Thus thirteen hearts are needed to balance scale c.

59

9	+	6	x	3	-	7	=	38
-		x		+		x		
3	x	9	+	7	-	6	=	28
x		-		x		-		
6	+	7	-	9	x	3	=	12
+		+		-		+		
7	-	3	x	6	+	9	=	33
=		=		=		=		
43		50		84		48		

60

1. Clubs
2. 2
3. 20: 4, 6, 9, and ace
4. 17: 5, jack, and ace
5. The 6 of hearts
6. 22: queen, 5, 4, and ace
7. Spades
8. The 8 of clubs

61

$$10 - 7 + 11 \times 4 \div 8 + 12 = 19$$

62

65

66

The center is very important. Try to restrict the movement of your opponent's coins (e.g., into a corner) so that there's more opportunity to make a winning line.

67

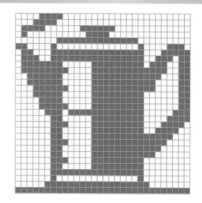

68

$$20 + 14 - 9 \times 6 - 18 \div 3 = 44$$

63

d; it contains five empty circles, whereas the other shields only contain four empty circles each.

64

329476; each number is the third, fourth, and fifth digits of the previous number reversed, followed by the first, second, and sixth digits of the previous number in the same order.

69

73; they are the digits of the three times table (3, 6, 9, 12, 15, 18, 21, 24, 27, 30) rearranged in groups of two.

70

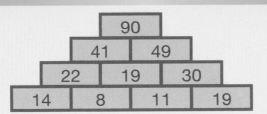

71

Seven minutes past ten. The hour hand points to the number of letters in the city's name. The minute hand points to the value of the first letter (i.e., 1 minute past equals A, 2 minutes past equals B, and so on).

GEORGETOWN

72

b; each vertical line and horizontal line contain two right-side-up pairs of lightning bolts and one inverted pair. Each line contains a black, a white, and a green central oval. Each line contains two green cages and one white wire cage over the oval. Finally, each line contains one image with two buttons, one with a single button, and one with no buttons. The missing image should have a pair of right-side-up lightning bolts and a white central oval with a green cage, and one button.

73

74

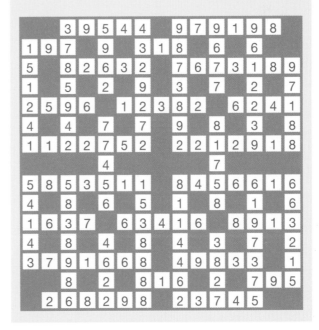

75

1. Orange
2. 9
3. Pink
4. Blue
5. 8
6. Blue, pink, and orange
7. 7
8. Purple

76

He does his patrols when his digital clock is displaying a palindromic time: 01:10, 02:20, 03:30, 04:40, 05:50, 10:01, 11:11, 12:21.

77

d; every fifth square contains a left diagonal line, every fourth square contains a red dot, and every third square contains a right diagonal line.

78

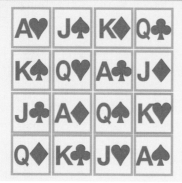

79

The combination is 81. Correct versions of false statements:

B. IQ stands for Intelligence Quotient.

E. The first Boeing 747 jumbo jet flew in February 1969.

H. A lepidopterist collects butterflies.

K. Omega is the final letter of the Greek alphabet.

N. Cygnus cygnus is the Latin classification for the swan.

80

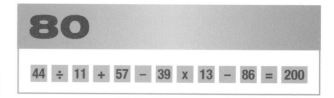

44 ÷ 11 + 57 − 39 x 13 − 86 = 200

81

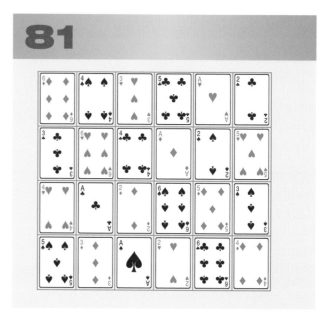

82

9263; all the others follow the pattern:
7421/2471
3869/6839
4283/8243
in which the first and third digits have swapped places.

83

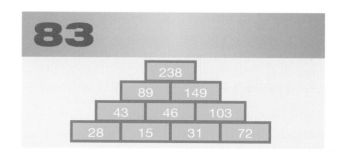

84

9731862; the numbers are rearranged so that all the odd numbers (in numerically descending order) are followed by all the even numbers (in numerically descending order).

85

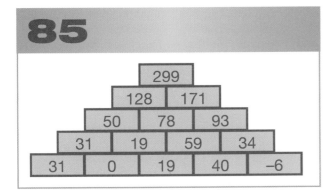

86

70 + 86 ÷ 13 x 66 ÷ 4 − 27 = 171

87

Wayne's second name is Brady. He isn't a center forward or a midfielder and he didn't score 1 goal (1). Darius didn't score 5 goals (1). Charlton plays for Rovers; he didn't score 1 goal, and Brady didn't score 5 (2). The center forward plays for Rangers and didn't score 5 or 4 goals (3). The Rovers' player, Charlton, didn't score 1 or 2 (3). Paul plays for United and didn't score 1 goal (4). Hughes scored 4 and isn't a winger (5). The left winger is Emile. He didn't score 1, 2, 5 (6), or 4 goals (5), so he must have scored 3. Callan didn't score 5 (7). Wayne Brady didn't score 1 (1), 5 (2), or 4 (5) goals. Emile scored 3, so Wayne must have scored 2. The Rangers' center forward didn't score 5, 4 (3), 3 (left winger), or 2 (Wayne Brady, not a center forward), so he scored 1. Paul scored one more than David, neither scored 2 (Wayne) or 3 (Emile) goals, so Paul must have scored 5 for United and David 4, leaving Darius with 1, which makes him the Rangers' center forward. The Rovers player scored two more than Darius (3), giving him 3 and making him Emile, in which case the Town player scored 4 (6). This leaves the City defender (7) with 2, making him Wayne Brady. Hughes scored 4 (5), so he's the Town player named David. Callan got 1 (7), making him Darius, the Rangers' center forward. Best then plays for United, making him Paul with 5 goals, and since neither Callan (center forward), Brady (defender), Hughes (5), nor Charlton (left wing) are right wingers, Paul Best must be one and David Hughes must be the midfielder for Town.

Wayne Brady—City—defender—2 goals
David Hughes—Town—midfield—4 goals
Paul Best—United—right wing—5 goals
Darius Callan—Rangers—center forward—1 goal
Emile Charlton—Rovers—left wing—3 goals

88

| 14 | x | 5 | + | 33 | − | 19 | ÷ | 4 | + | 15 | = | 36 |

89

3527; in all of the others, the sum of the first two digits is equal to the sum of the second two digits, e.g., 3984, where 3 + 9 = 8 + 4.

90

8; one knife and one fork weigh as much as six spoons, so two knives and one fork weigh as much as five forks. Thus one knife weighs as much as two forks. Three forks thus balance six spoons and one fork balances two spoons. Thus eight spoons are needed to balance scale c.

91

92

To decode, you type the message on the keyboard but move your fingers one key to the left each time. For example, a W becomes a Q instead. The deciphered message reads as follows: "The code word is a city in New York state, which is described as a bison in the US." Therefore, the code word is BUFFALO.

93

6947; reverse the digits and discard the smallest value digit each time.

94

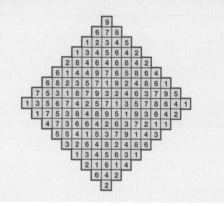

95

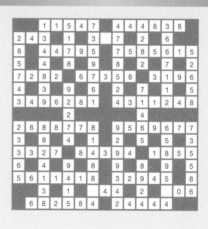

96

1217; 5 + 7 = 12; 9 + 8 = 17

97

Cards that have moved are shown shaded.

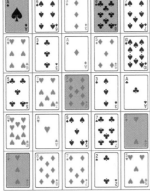

98

Bobby is Bobby Macfie and he played marbles. Bobby Macfie wasn't 4th or 5th and he and the marbles were not on the soccer field (1). The 3rd place finisher was in the common room, and it wasn't Wendy nor Betsy (2). The 4th place was hopscotch, not Wendy nor Betsy nor with the last name Stuart (3). The Hacky Sack player was not named Stuart and not 5th, and jump rope wasn't 1st (4). Wendy was in the playground. She isn't Macdonald or Macfie (5). Betsy is Betsy Campbell, wasn't 1st, didn't play hopscotch, and wasn't in the cafeteria (6). Billy was 1st, but not in Hacky Sack, marbles, nor on the soccer field (7). Billy wasn't 4th, and neither was Bobby (1), Wendy, nor Betsy (3), so it must have been William and he must have been playing hopscotch (3). Jump rope was in the quad and not done by William, Billy, or Bobby (8). Hacky Sack wasn't Billy, Betsy, or Bobby, or played in the cafeteria or common room (9). Hacky Sack, marbles (7), jump rope (4), and hopscotch (3) weren't 1st, so jacks must have been, and jacks must be Billy (7). Betsy wasn't then jacks nor hopscotch (6), marbles (1), nor Hacky Sack (9), so she must have been jumping rope in the quad (8). Wendy wasn't skipping then, and she wasn't playing hopscotch (3), marbles (1), or jacks (Billy), so she must be Hacky Sack. Hacky Sack finished higher than jump rope (4), neither were 1st (7 & 4) or 4th (3), jump rope wasn't 3rd (2), and so Hacky Sack was 2nd and jump rope was 5th (Betsy Campbell in the quad), leaving marbles with 3rd—in the common room (2) with Bobby Macfie (1). Stuart isn't marbles (1), Hacky Sack (4), hopscotch (3), nor jump rope (Betsy Campbell), so must be jacks and thus 1st and Billy. Wendy isn't Macfie (1), Campbell (6), Macdonald, nor Macfie, so she must be Lewis and William must be Macdonald. So:
Bobby Macfie—3rd—common room—marbles
Billy Stuart—1st—cafeteria—jacks
Wendy Lewis—2nd—playground—Hacky Sack
Betsy Campbell—5th—quad—jump rope
William Macdonald—4th—soccer field—hopscotch.

99

13 + 27 ÷ 10 + 15 − 11 x 9 = 72

100

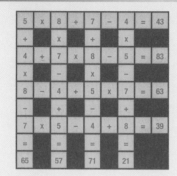

101

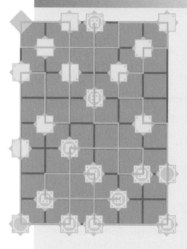

The solution path starts and finishes with the full design: first visiting designs that have had one element removed until just a background shape remains, then replacing the elements until the design is once more complete.

102

When choosing a word, remember that words with a small number of vowels will be more difficult to guess. Examples of five-letter words with no vowels include DRYLY, HYMNS, NYMPH, and TRYST. Do not change your guesses too radically otherwise you will find it difficult to figure out the logic. If you can, move one letter and change another letter completely.

103

d; each vertical and horizontal line contains two white pigs and a pink one. Each line contains two pink-nosed pigs and a white-nosed pig. Each line contains a pig with black feet, a pig with white feet, and a pig with pink feet. Each line contains two pigs with four spots and one with three spots. Each line has two pigs facing left and one facing right. Finally, each line contains two pigs with a tail and one with no tail. The missing pig should be white, with a white nose, white feet, four spots, be facing left, and have a tail.

104

2634 and 16; the two-figure numbers in the top group are the sum of the digits of each of the four-figure numbers in the bottom group and vice versa. For example, 7529/23 (7 + 5 + 2 + 9 = 23).

105

M minutes per mile = (60/M) mph = (60 x 1.6/M) km/h = M km/h. This simplifies to M being the square root of 96 (approx. 9.8). In other words, around 9.8 minutes per mile is the same rate as 9.8 km/h.

106

	119		
	53	66	
	24	29	37
11.5	12.5	16.5	20.5
3	8.5	4	12.5	8

107

17
05
Looking across at numbers in the same position in each block, the series of numbers progress: 7, 5, 3, 1, (–2); 4, 5, 6, 7 (+1); 9, 6, 3, 0 (–3); 8, 7, 6, 5 (–1).

108

109

110

1	8	15	10
11	14	5	4
6	3	12	13
16	9	2	7

111

13	+	12	x	25	–	16	=	609
+		x		–		+		
25	–	16	x	12	+	13	=	121
–		+		+		x		
12	x	13	+	16	–	25	=	147
x		–		x		–		
16	+	25	–	13	x	12	=	336
=		=		=		=		
416		180		377		713		

112

92 and 81; in all the others the number at the bottom is produced by taking the second digit of the top number less 1, followed by the first digit of the top number less 1.

113

Strangely, the only possible solution turns out to be 9:48. This works because the hour hand moves one "tick" clockwise after every 12 minutes. At 9 o'clock, the hour hand is 45 ticks around the clock. At 9:48, it will be 49 ticks around, and the minute hand will be at the 48th tick. Therefore, the hands are exactly one tick apart.

114

c; rotate the grid 90 degrees clockwise, then deduct 1 from the odd numbers and add 1 to the even numbers.

115

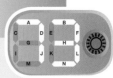

The combination is 73. Correct versions of false statements:
C. In heraldry, the color green is referred to as vert.
E. The 1984 Olympic Games were held in Los Angeles.
G. Don Quixote's horse was named Rosinante.
I. Tia Maria is a liqueur flavored with coffee.
K. "As old as time itself" is an example of a simile.

M. Coryza is the scientific name for the common cold.

116

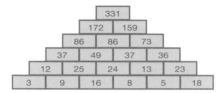

Decipher the bottom row using the system A = 1, B = 2, C = 3, etc., which spells out the word CIPHER.

117

19.5; the sequence progresses: divide by 3/add 3/multiply by 3/ subtract 3.

118

6589; in all the others the number formed by the middle two digits is the product (multiplied together) of the first and last digits, for example, 8567, where 8 x 7 = 56.

119

80; subtract 0.5, then 1.5, then 4.5, then 13.5, i.e., the amount subtracted is multiplied by 3 each time.

120

1. Carol
2. An 8
3. Ella (card values total 37)
4. Adam and John (card values total 25)
5. 2
6. George
7. John
8. Spades

121

25 x 15 − 87 ÷ 12 + 79 + 44 = 147

122

The top three levels are straightforward. For the other numbers we need to employ a different approach. One method is to replace the three unknowns with the letters A, B, and C. This gives us these three equations:
$65 = (9 + A) + (A + B)$, hence $2A + B = 56$;
$98 = (A + B) + (B + C)$, hence $A + 2B + C = 98$;
$110 = (B + C) + (C + 14)$, hence $B + 2C = 96$.
Adding the first and last equation together gives $2A + 2B + 2C = 152$, hence $A + B + C = 76$.

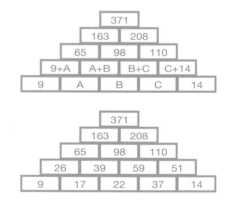

Comparing this with the middle equation shows that B must be 22, since it has another B and its total is 22 higher. Now that we know B = 22, it's easy to see that A = 17 and C = 37 from the other equations. The rest of the pyramid can now be completed.

123

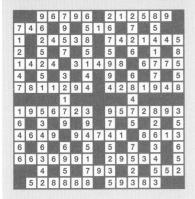

124

d; each vertical and horizontal line contains a green, a blue, and a red umbrella. Each line contains a brown, a black, and a gray briefcase. Each line contains two black hats and a blue one. Each line contains two pairs of sneakers with dark blue stripes and one pair with red stripes. Each line contains one image with missing cuff buttons. Finally, each line has one of the three images facing right. The missing image should have a green umbrella, a gray suitcase, a black hat, blue striped sneakers, and cuff buttons and should be facing right.

125

Square 1 goes in position D, 2 to A, 3 to C, and 4 to B.

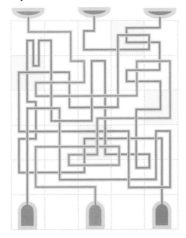

126

With an odd number of coins, making moves that are the mirror-image to your opponent's will guarantee a win.

127

8 p.m.; since this is one hour later than the midpoint between 1 p.m and 1 a.m., namely 7 p.m.

128

d, 191029; in all the others, add the first two numbers to produce the number formed by the third and fourth digits, then add again to produce the number formed by the fifth and sixth digits. For example 3 + 9 = 12, and 9 +12 = 21, this producing the number 391221. Option d, following this rule, should be 191019, not 191029.

129

5	11	8	10
4	14	1	15
9	7	12	6
16	2	13	3

130

Here is one possible solution:

		3		
	7		4	
	2	9	5	
8	10	1	6	

131

8132479; the positions of the numbers move as follows:

A	B	C	D	E	F	G
7	2	9	6	3	8	4
6	1	7	4	2	5	8
2	9	1	7	8	3	4

E	C	F	A	G	D	B
3	9	8	7	4	6	2
2	7	5	6	8	4	1
8	1	3	2	4	7	9

ACKNOWLEDGMENTS ✪ DEDUCTIVE PUZZLES

✪ **Puzzle contributors**

Contributors are listed next to the numbers of the puzzles they created.

✪ **David Bodycombe**

Puzzles 1, 2, 3, 10, 11, 14, 15, 19, 28, 38, 41, 42, 48, 50, 56, 66, 70, 71, 73, 76, 78, 79, 83, 85, 91, 92, 102, 105, 106, 110, 113, 115, 116, 122, 126, 127, 129, 130

✪ **Guy Campbell**

Puzzles 8, 12, 16, 17, 24, 26, 40, 44, 51, 53, 54, 57, 67, 72, 87, 98, 101, 103, 109, 124, 125

✪ **Philip Carter**

Puzzles 4, 13, 23, 27, 30, 31, 39, 46, 47, 63, 64, 69, 77, 82, 84, 89, 93, 96, 104, 107, 112, 114, 117, 118, 119, 128, 131

✪ **Probyn Puzzles**

Puzzles 5, 6, 7, 21, 25, 32, 34, 35, 49, 52, 59, 61, 62, 68, 74, 80, 86, 88, 95, 99, 100, 108, 111, 121, 123

✪ **Puzzler Media Ltd**

Puzzles 9, 18, 20, 22, 29, 33, 36, 37, 43, 45, 55, 58, 60, 65, 75, 81, 90, 94, 97, 120

Deductive Puzzles was commissioned, edited, designed, and produced by:
Book Creation Ltd., 20 Lochaline Street, London W6 9SH, United Kingdom
Managing Director: Hal Robinson
Editor: David Popey **Art Editor:** Keith Miller
Designer: Justin Hunt **Copy Editor:** Sarah Barlow **Editorial Assistants:** Claire Bratt, Rosemary Browne

Numeric Puzzles

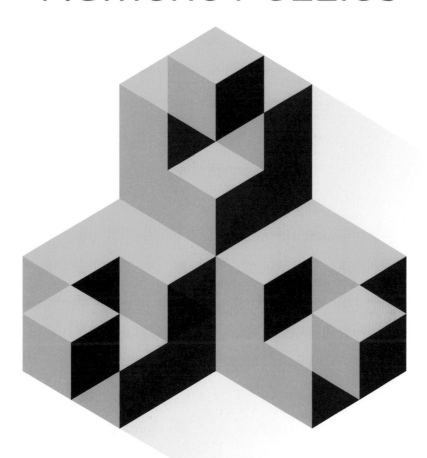

**N**umeric Puzzles is a compilation of puzzles for anyone who wants to maximize their mental arithmetic skills and sharpen their numerical "intuition."

No matter what your level of ability, a carefully graded series of challenges ensures that this section will have plenty for you.

The relationship between words and numbers is curious—words and numbers are both handled by the left hemisphere of the human brain and processed in the same way, regardless of their seeming differences. There are ten digits and twenty-six letters, yet numbers are infinite while the variety of words is finite. In spite of the fact that number puzzles use only ten digits along with the four basic mathematical operations (and perhaps the occasional square root or two), there is an amazing variety to be found in the world of number puzzles. Before you know it, you'll be completing sequences in a flash, dashing through the most difficult divisions, and scaling the heights of our number pyramids.

Traditional formats for word-based puzzles, such as crosswords and word searches, also get their own numeric treatments.

Each puzzle in *Numeric Puzzles* has been carefully graded according to a ten-star system—the more stars there are, the harder that puzzle will be. Remember that these ratings are based on an average performance, so don't be surprised if you breeze through a ten-star stumper (or are baffled by a three-star puzzler!) But it doesn't end there—since speed of calculation is just as important as accuracy, every challenge has been given its own time limit for you to work toward.

There are no sneaky tricks here. You don't need to know logarithms, calculus, or group theory (or even know what they mean). All of the puzzles are based on straightforward operations, although some are better disguised than others. If you find that you can't crunch through a particular calculation, the answers section at the back of this section will provide you with the solution. Every question in this section has been numbered—simply refer to the same number in the answer section and all will be revealed. But have one last attempt at solving the problem before resorting to the solutions, since the satisfaction of cracking a seemingly impossible problem is its own reward.

By the end of *Numeric Puzzles*, having honed your skills on these mathematical puzzles, you'll find yourself seeing numerical relationships and solving mathematical problems more quickly and easily than you ever imagined ●

—Alison Moore

1 DIFFICULTY ★★★★★★☆☆☆☆
Target time: 5 minutes

Can you place the tiles in the grid so that:

* each row and column contains two squares of each color, and

* each row and column contains exactly one of each number?

2 DIFFICULTY ★★★★☆☆☆☆☆
Target time: 8 minutes

Can you fit these numbers into the grid? One number has already been inserted to help you get started.

34749

3 Digits
690
811

4 Digits
1305
2466
3268
5396
6316
6578
7173
7290

5 Digits
10743
14920
27626
~~34749~~
51349

61623
73811
80753
92607
94742

6 Digits
115800
432836

787418
874644

7 Digits
1193788
1736453
2402326
3193210
3241096

3529493
4687333
4698382
5359681
5621599
6480183
6734967
7341442
8914913

3 DIFFICULTY ●●●✩✩✩✩✩✩✩
Target time: 3 minutes

Make a calculation totaling the figure on the right, and using some or all of the numbers on the left with any of the four standard mathematical operators (+, −, x, and ÷).

3, 4, 5, 8, 9, 25 = 527

4 DIFFICULTY ●●●●●●●✩✩✩
Target time: 5 minutes

Study these balloons carefully for one minute, then answer the questions on the next page without checking back.

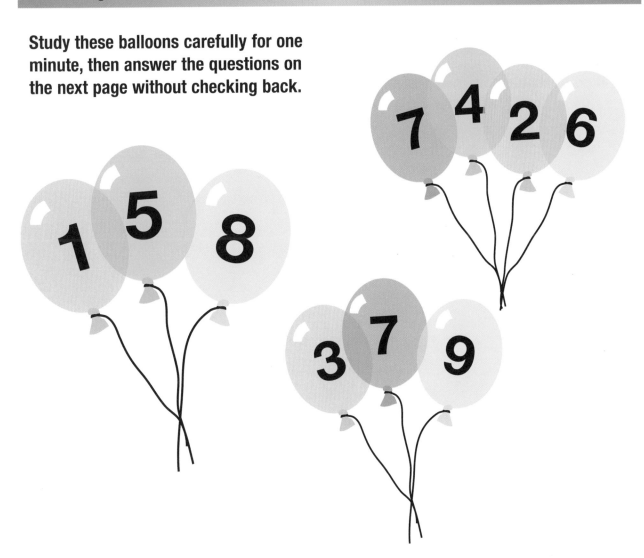

[4] DIFFICULTY ★★★★★☆☆☆☆☆
Target time: 5 minutes

Can you answer these questions about the puzzle on the previous page without checking back?

1. The numbers on two bunches of balloons add up to the same figure. What is it?

2. What's the total of the numbers on the pink balloons?

3. Which number appears twice?

4. On which colored balloons does it appear?

5. How many pink balloons have odd numbers?

6. Which odd number appears on a blue balloon?

7. Which even number appears on a yellow balloon?

8. How many balloons are green?

5 DIFFICULTY ★★★★★☆☆☆☆☆
Target time: 3 minutes

Which clock face is the odd one out?

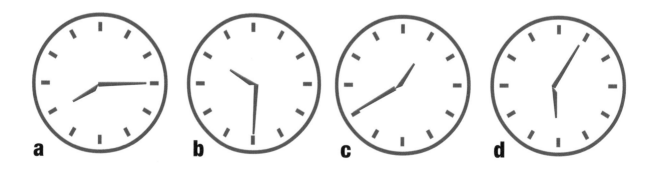

a   b   c   d

6 DIFFICULTY ✪✪✪✪✪☆☆☆☆☆
Target time: 10 minutes

Starting with the yellow square on the top left corner, find the path through the squares, calculating each step to lead you to the solution on the bottom right corner. You may not pass through the same square more than once.

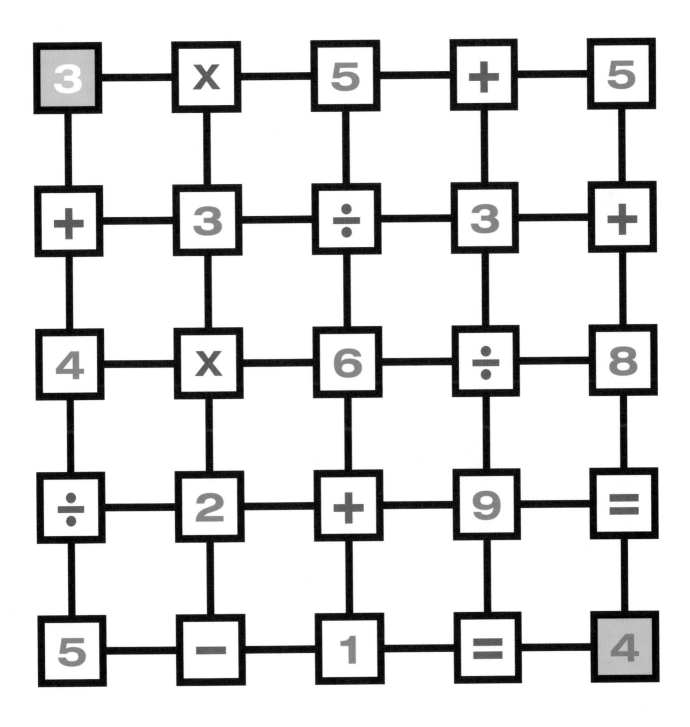

7 DIFFICULTY ✪✪✪✪✪☆☆☆☆☆
Target time: 3 minutes

Consider the apples, bananas, and oranges shown below. Given that scales a and b balance perfectly, how many apples are needed to balance scale c?

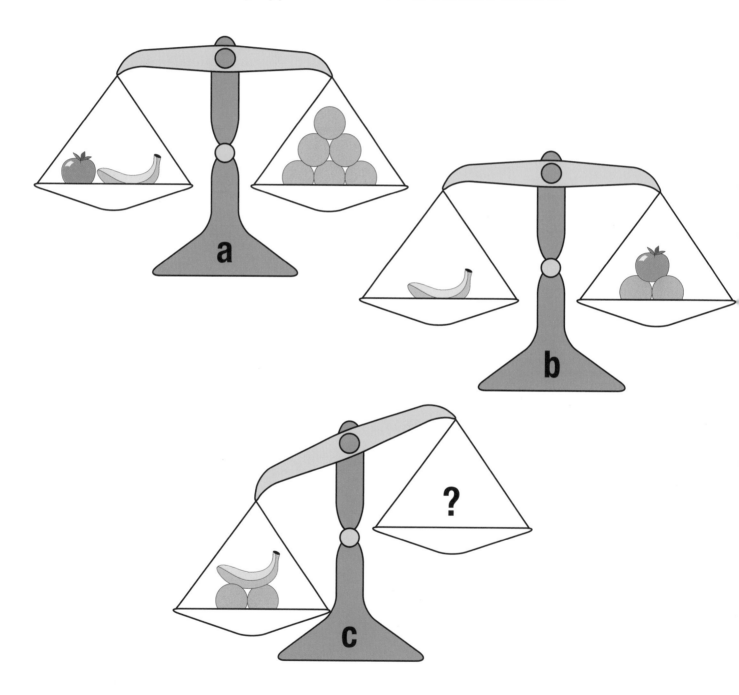

8 DIFFICULTY ●●●●●☆☆☆☆☆

Target time: 8 minutes

Find the solutions to the following calculations in the grid, reading up, down, backward, forward, and diagonally!

1. 9 x 9 x 9 x 9
2. (40 x 40) + 400
3. (100 − 44) x 22
4. 8,989 + 1,111
5. 77 + 88 + 88 + 99
6. 1,234 x 5
7. 44 x 66

8. 666 + 334
9. 8,765 − 1,111
10. (9 + 9) x 99
11. (10,000 ÷ 20) + 20
12. 90,990 ÷ 3
13. (565 x 2) x 2

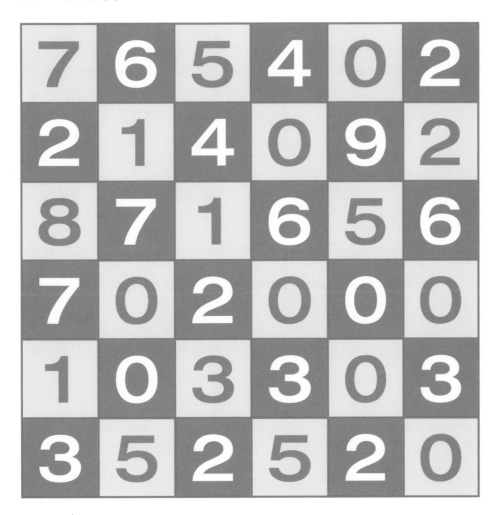

9 DIFFICULTY ★★★★☆☆☆☆☆☆
Target time: 6 minutes

Every row and column contains the same numbers and signs, but they are arranged in a different order each time. Find the correct order to arrive at the final totals shown.

3	+	2	x	6	−	5	=	25
							=	17
							=	27
							=	24
=		=		=		=		
21		7		9		15		

10 DIFFICULTY ✪✪✪✪✪☆☆☆☆☆

Target time: 5 minutes

This is a two-player game. Players take turns removing as many coins as they like from one of the three rows. If you pick up the last coin, you lose the game. Once you've played the game a few times, see if you can work out how to guarantee a win by starting first.

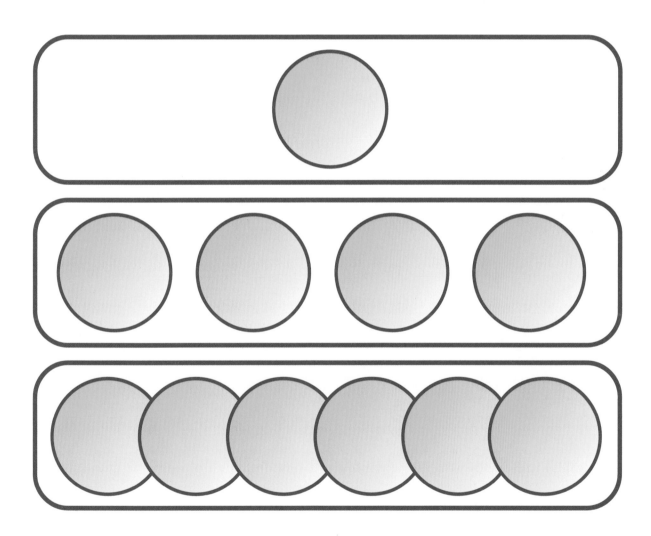

11 DIFFICULTY ★★★★☆☆☆☆☆☆
Target time: 4 minutes

The number 543,789 appears just once in this grid and occurs in a straight line, running either backward or forward in a horizontal, vertical, or diagonal direction. Can you locate it?

5	4	3	7	9	8	7	3	5	4	9	5
9	8	3	5	9	3	7	5	3	4	8	4
3	4	7	5	4	3	5	9	5	3	7	7
4	5	4	9	4	5	8	4	7	3	9	3
5	4	3	7	9	3	3	8	5	9	8	8
9	3	4	8	5	7	9	9	4	9	9	9
4	7	9	4	9	8	9	7	7	3	4	5
8	5	9	5	4	3	5	8	9	8	8	3
7	9	5	3	5	9	8	7	3	4	5	9
5	1	4	7	4	8	7	5	9	7	5	3
8	5	3	5	3	3	4	9	5	8	4	4
9	8	7	3	5	4	5	4	3	9	7	8

12 DIFFICULTY ✪✪✪✪✪✪✩✩✩✩
Target time: 10 minutes

Can you fit these numbers into the grid? One number has already been inserted to help you get started.

3 Digits
315
877

4 Digits
1572
1821
2594
2680
2757
7263
7425
9484

5 Digits
20901
24443
30405
32850
51215
71044
73214
75159
76154
~~97492~~

6 Digits
115695
739715
828736
942829

7 Digits
1419694

2586646
4948087
5645235
6029257
6048933
6498877
6817511
7472517

7647885
7776672
7972733
9461031
9877768

9 7 4 9 2

13 DIFFICULTY ★★★★★★★★★★☆

Target time: 30 minutes

If you like nonograms, this one should suit you!

HOW TO DO A NONOGRAM:

Along each row or column there are numbers that indicate how many blocks of black squares are in a line. For example, "3, 4, 5" indicates that from left to right or top to bottom, there is a group of three black squares, then a group of four black squares, then another group of five black squares.

Each block of black squares on the same line must have at least one white square between it and the next block of black squares. Blocks of black squares may or may not have a number of white squares before and after them.

It is sometimes possible to determine which squares will be black without reference to other lines or columns. It is helpful to put a small dot in a square you know will be empty.

Column clues:

																				2	4		4	2					
					2	3		3	2											3	1		1	3					
	3	2	1	1	3	2	5	2	3	1	1	2	3			1	3	5	5	1	2	13	2	1	5	5	3	1	
	7	6	5	4	8	9	1	9	8	4	5	6	7			7	6	5	4	3	2	1	2	3	4	5	6	7	
15	4	6	7	8	1	2	13	2	1	8	7	6	4	15	15	7	6	5	4	3	2	1	2	3	4	5	6	7	15

Row clues:

				15
	3	5	3	1
	2	3	2	3
	1	1	1	5
	1	1	1	5
		1	1	3
1	1	2	1	2
1	1	4	1	4
		2	2	13
	3		1	
4		2	1	2
		5	5	1
		6	6	3
		7	7	5
				15
				15
		1	7	7
		3	6	6
		5	5	5
		7	4	4
		9	3	3
		11	2	2
		13	1	1
		13	2	2
		13	3	3
		13	4	4
3	1	3	5	5
		3	6	6
		5	7	7
				15

14 DIFFICULTY ●●●●●★★★★★★

Target time: 4 minutes

Each block is equal to the sum of the two numbers
beneath it. Find all the missing numbers.

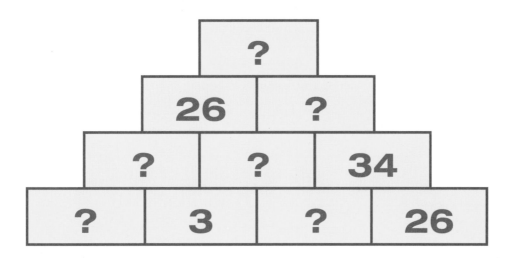

15 DIFFICULTY ●●●●●●★★★★★

Target time: 4 minutes

These four points
are the corners
of a square. If a
has coordinates
of (4, 5), and c is
at (10, 1), what are
the coordinates
of b and d?

a ●

● b

● c

d ●

16 DIFFICULTY ✪✪✪✪☆☆☆☆☆☆
Target time: 3 minutes

Which is the odd number out?

159, 367, 589, 258, 486, 679

17 DIFFICULTY ✪✪✪✪☆☆☆☆☆☆
Target time: 4 minutes

Replace the question marks with mathematical symbols to produce the correct answer. Only the four basic operators (+, −, x, and ÷) are permitted. Perform calculations in strict left to right order. Can you find two possible solutions?

6 ? 2 ? 2 ? 3 ? 7

= 16

18 DIFFICULTY ✪✪✪✪☆☆☆☆☆☆
Target time: 4 minutes

Can you place the tiles in the grid so that:

* each row and column contains two squares of each color, and
* no row or column contains more than one of any number?

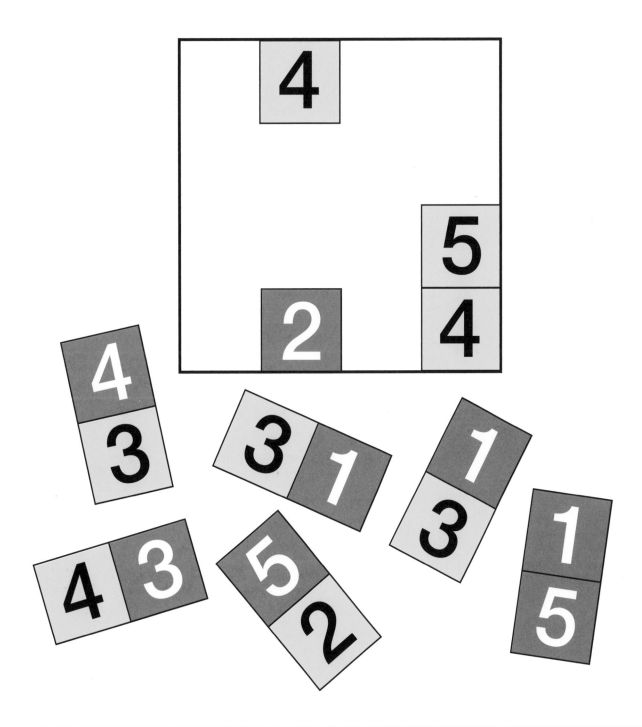

19 DIFFICULTY ✪✪✪✪☆☆☆☆☆☆
Target time: 3 minutes

Place a number in the middle box that divides into all the other numbers without leaving a remainder. The answer is greater than 1.

273		126
231		168
147		252

20 DIFFICULTY ✪✪✪✪✪☆☆☆☆☆
Target time: 3 minutes

At a local club, a dice game is played that involves throwing two dice and betting a stake of $5. What are the rules, and how much did Gary Gambler win or lose when he threw a 5, followed by a 2? Study the clues below to discover the answer!

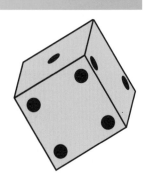

1. Gina threw a 4, followed by a 4, and lost her whole stake. She paid another stake and tried again. This time she threw a 3, followed by a 1, and got $6 back, thus winning $1 on her second try.

2. George threw a 6, followed by a 2, and got $12 back, so won $7.

3. Grant threw a 1, followed by a 3, and got $6 back, so won $1.

21 DIFFICULTY ✪✪✪✪✪✪✩✩✩
Target time: 5 minutes

Given that scales a and b balance perfectly, how many suns are needed to balance scale c?

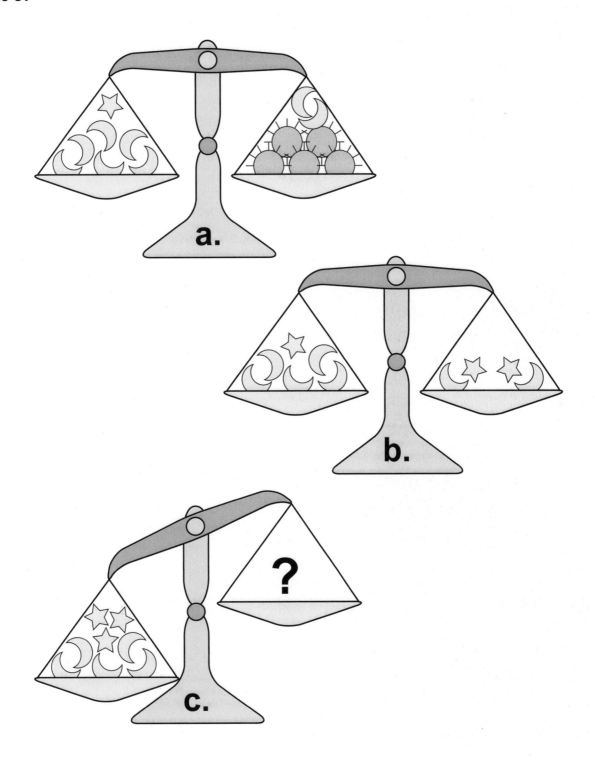

22 DIFFICULTY ✪✪✪✪☆☆☆☆☆☆
Target time: 3 minutes

What number should replace the question mark in the following sequence?

100, 98.75, 96.25, 95, 92.5, ?

23 DIFFICULTY ✪✪✪✪✪☆☆☆☆☆
Target time: 4 minutes

Find out the mystery sequence hidden in the dominoes, then decide which number should replace the question mark.

a  = 34

b  = 51

c  = 71

d  = ?

24 DIFFICULTY ✪✪✪✪✪✪☆☆☆☆
Target time: 6 minutes

Can you divide this square into four equally shaped parts of nine smaller squares, each containing two different numbers and two different shapes?

25 DIFFICULTY ✪✪✪✪✪✪✪✪☆☆
Target time: 8 minutes

And now can you divide this square into four identical shapes, each composed of sixteen squares, and each containing four different numbers?

26 DIFFICULTY ✪✪✪✪☆☆☆✪☆☆
Target time: 4 minutes

Which domino (a, b, c, or d) should fill the empty space?

  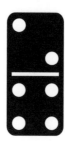 

a **b** **c** **d**

27 DIFFICULTY ✪✪✪✪☆☆☆✪☆☆
Target time: 3 minutes

Place a number in the middle box that divides into all the other numbers without leaving a remainder. The answer is greater than 1.

102		442
136		561
187		306

28 DIFFICULTY ✪✪✪✪✪✩✩✩✩✩
Target time: 5 minutes

Each block is equal to the sum of the two numbers beneath it.
Find all the missing numbers.

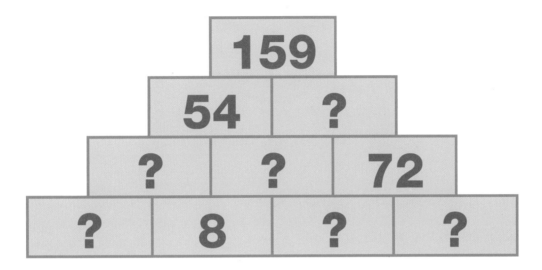

29 DIFFICULTY ✪✪✪✪✩✩✩✩✩✩
Target time: 3 minutes

Which is the odd number out?

1,235   *2,134*

3,145   *4,268*

5,279   *4,569*

30 DIFFICULTY ★★★☆☆☆☆☆☆☆
Target time: 3 minutes

What time should come next on clock e?

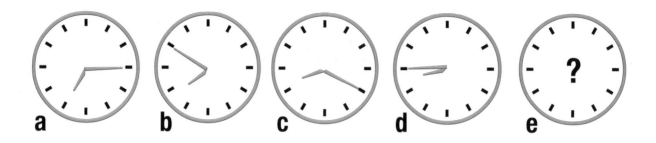

a   b   c   d   e

31 DIFFICULTY ★★★★☆☆☆☆☆☆
Target time: 4 minutes

Replace the question marks with mathematical symbols to produce the correct answer. Only the four basic operators (+, −, x, and ÷) are permitted. Perform calculations in strict left to right order. Can you find two possible solutions?

$$12 \; ? \; 4 \; ? \; 7$$

$$? \; 8 = 7$$

32 DIFFICULTY ★★★★☆☆☆☆☆☆
Target time: 6 minutes

Can you fit these numbers into the grid? One number has already been given to help you get started.

3 Digits
544
675

4 Digits
2534
3145
4812
4983
5343
6911
7403
9462

5 Digits
20010
~~35041~~
46255
57193
57488

69606
74366
81587
87449
92579

6 Digits
379253
681202

813024
916115

7 Digits
1712470
2041019
3496883
3756076
4099359

4109509
4549428
5179153
6015117
7810067
7895619
8107408
8589334
9264533

33 DIFFICULTY ✪✪✪✪✪✪✪☆✰☆

Target time: 5 minutes

Weigh up the symbols below. Given that scales a and b balance perfectly, how many clubs are needed to balance scale c?

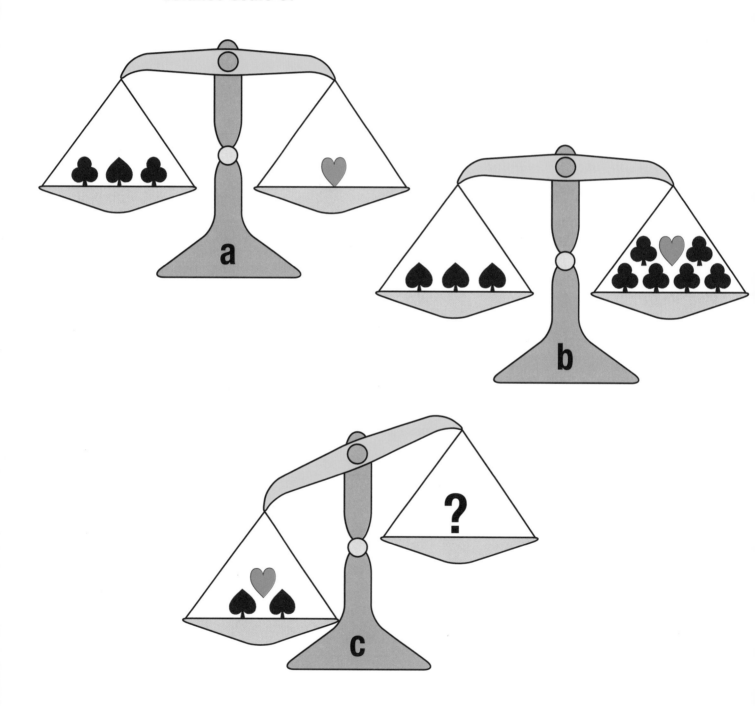

34 DIFFICULTY ✪✪✪✪✪✩✩✩✩✩✩
Target time: 3 minutes

Which number is the odd one out?

17 **37** **61**

23 **42** **59**

35 DIFFICULTY ✪✪✪✪✪✩✩✩✩✩✩
Target time: 3 minutes

At the local club, a dice game is played that involves throwing two dice and betting a stake of $12. What are the rules—and how much did Gary Gambler win or lose when he threw a 4, followed by a 5? Study the clues below to discover the answer!

1. Gina threw a 2, followed by a 2, and got $4 back, losing $8.

2. George threw a 6, followed by a 2, and broke even, so got $12 back.

3. Grant threw a 1, followed by a 3, and got $3 back, so lost $9.

Find the answers to the following calculations in the grid, reading up, down, backward, forward, and diagonally.

1. 54,321 – 12,345
2. 15 x 15 x 15
3. 909 + 707
4. 55,000 ÷ 25
5. 11,111 + 12,345
6. 2,727 ÷ 9
7. (6,204 ÷ 2) ÷ 2
8. 10,000 – 4,445
9. 3,108 ÷ 7
10. 5 x 5 x 5 x 5 x 5
11. 15 x 51
12. 999 – 343

2	2	0	0	4	4
3	0	3	1	4	7
6	5	9	4	6	5
1	7	1	5	5	1
6	3	6	5	6	6
1	3	5	2	1	3

37 DIFFICULTY ⭐⭐⭐⭐⭐✩✩✩✩✩
Target time: 4 minutes

Study these shapes for one minute, then see if you can answer the questions that follow on the next page without checking back.

38 DIFFICULTY ⭐⭐⭐⭐⭐⭐⭐✩✩✩
Target time: 6 minutes

What theorem do these two diagrams prove?

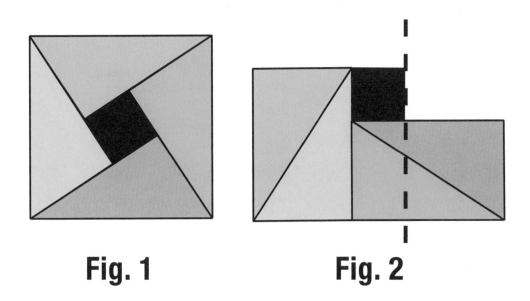

Fig. 1   **Fig. 2**

[37] DIFFICULTY ✪✪✪✪✪✩✩✩✩✩
Target time: 4 minutes

Can you answer these questions about the puzzle on the previous page without checking back?

1. How many shapes have prime numbers?
2. Which two numbers will total a third number shown?
3. What is the total when you multiply the number on the blue shape by that on the pink shape?
4. Which shapes have odd numbers?
5. Which colors have even numbers?
6. What is the total reached by adding the number on the yellow shape to that on the square, then subtracting this total from the number on the shape on the far right?

39 DIFFICULTY ✪✪✪✩✩✩✩✩✩✩
Target time: 3 minutes

Make a calculation totaling the figure at the bottom using some or all of the numbers in the box with any of the four standard mathematical operators (+, −, x, and ÷).

$$4 \ ? \ 4 \ ? \ 6 \ ?$$

$$7 \ ? \ 9 \ ? \ 10$$

$$= 311$$

40 DIFFICULTY ★★★★☆☆☆☆☆☆
Target time: 6 minutes

The number 1,899,740 appears just once in this number-search grid and occurs in a straight line, running either backward or forward in a horizontal, vertical, or diagonal direction. Can you find it?

1	8	0	4	8	7	0	9	1	8	0	4
4	7	8	0	9	8	1	9	9	8	1	0
4	1	0	0	7	9	8	9	1	7	4	0
7	8	9	0	1	4	7	0	9	1	9	8
4	9	0	4	7	8	4	8	1	0	7	7
8	9	8	7	0	9	0	8	9	0	0	9
9	0	7	9	4	8	9	1	4	9	0	4
8	8	4	9	8	1	9	4	9	7	8	9
1	0	7	8	4	9	0	1	8	9	4	9
9	7	9	1	4	0	1	8	0	9	8	0
4	9	8	0	8	4	0	8	1	4	7	8
8	7	1	1	4	1	9	8	7	9	1	1

41 DIFFICULTY ✪✪✪✪✪✪✪☆☆

Target time: 8 minutes

Can you divide this square into four identical shapes, each composed of sixteen squares, and each containing four different numbers?

			3	3			
		1					
		1		2		1	1
				4	4	2	
2	2						3
	4						3
	4						

42 DIFFICULTY ✪✪✪✪✪✪✪☆☆

Target time: 6 minutes

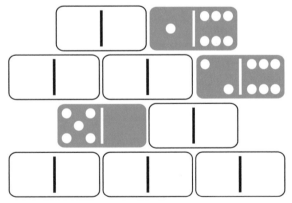

Ten dominoes have been used to build this wall, but seven have been masked out. Can you place the missing dominoes correctly, bearing in mind that each vertical line of four numbers (as well as the two end vertical lines of two numbers) adds up to eight?

43 DIFFICULTY ✪✪✪✪✪✩✩✩✩✩
Target time: 3 minutes

Place a number in the middle box that divides into all the other numbers without leaving a remainder. The answer is greater than 1.

132   143

121   154

165   209

44 DIFFICULTY ✪✪✪✪✪✪✩✩✩✩
Target time: 3 minutes

Which of these is the odd number out?

17, 71, 88, 88, 176, 671, 846

45 DIFFICULTY ✪✪✪✪✪✪✪☆☆

Target time: 8 minutes

Traverse this maze from top to bottom (any entry point on the top row may be used). You may only move from a number divisible by 5 to one divisible by 6, from a number divisible by 6 to one divisible by 7, or from one divisible by 7 to one divisible by 5. You may not move diagonally.

66	14	18	65	26	55	19
77	50	21	16	49	24	63
75	33	37	78	40	54	10
96	98	96	25	18	15	36
31	20	36	49	54	50	56
98	48	11	23	91	72	56
20	28	45	78	91	15	72
12	23	54	77	85	95	21
16	25	24	66	14	91	40

46 DIFFICULTY ✪✪✪✪✪✪✪✪✪✩
Target time: 30 minutes

Nonograms make good games. You will be bowled over by this one.
(See puzzle 13 for advice on how to complete a nonogram.)

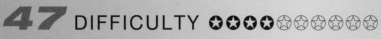

47 DIFFICULTY ★★★★☆☆☆☆☆☆

Target time: 4 minutes

Each block is equal to the sum of the two numbers beneath it. Find all the missing numbers.

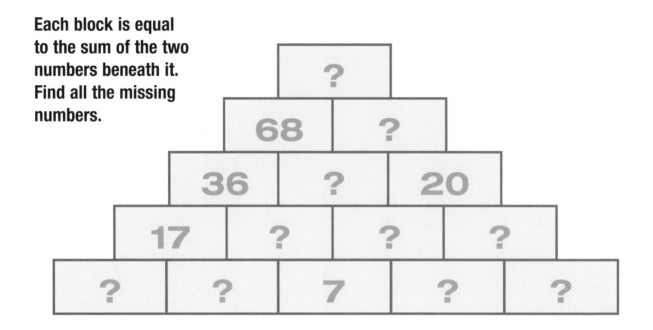

48 DIFFICULTY ★★★★★☆☆☆☆☆

Target time: 3 minutes

Which number should replace the question mark in the following sequence?

10, 5, 12, 6, 16, 9, 22, ?

49 DIFFICULTY ✪✪✪✪✪✪✪☆☆
Target time: 6 minutes

Place the pieces from a standard set of twenty-eight dominoes into the following grid by matching their numbers with those in the rectangle. It's trickier than you think, so we've placed one in position to give you a start and supplied a checklist on the right that may help!

3	6	5	5	6	1	3
5	5	0	2	2	4	3
4	4	6	1	0	0	0
1	0	0	1	4	2	5
1	0	1	5	1	4	5
2	3	3	0	2	6	2
6	3	4	2	4	6	3
6	3	4	6	1	2	5

0/0	0/1	0/2	0/3	0/4	0/5	0/6
1/1	1/2	1/3	1/4	1/5	1/6	2/2
2/3	2/4	2/5	2/6	3/3	3/4	3/5
3/6	4/4	4/5	4/6	5/5	5/6	6/6

50 DIFFICULTY ✪✪✪✪✪✪☆☆☆☆
Target time: 6 minutes

			3	1			
3	5				4	5	
	1		2	4		2	
			3		1		
5					4		4
	2	3		5		1	
						2	

Can you divide this square into four identical shapes, each composed of sixteen smaller squares, and each containing five different numbers?

51 DIFFICULTY ✪✪✪✪✪✪✪✪☆☆
Target time: 5 minutes

Using three of the four different mathematical operators beneath each of the following three sums, can you achieve the correct totals, as given?

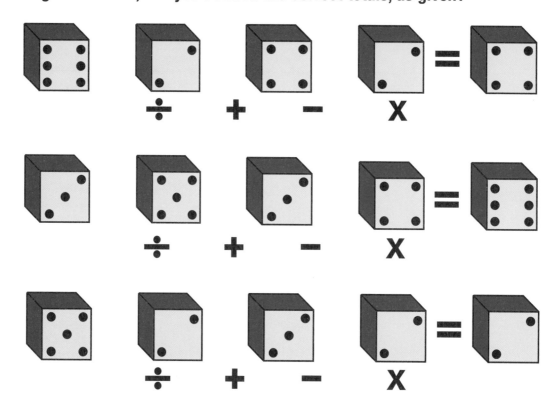

52 DIFFICULTY ✪✪✪✪✪✪☆☆☆☆
Target time: 3 minutes

Which is the odd number out?

2,743   2,917   9,461

9,172   6,813   4,819

3,724   1,836   9,418

53 DIFFICULTY ✪✪✪✪✪✪✪☆☆

Target time: 5 minutes

Fill in the missing number.

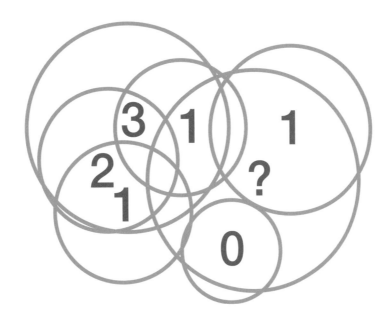

54 DIFFICULTY ✪✪✪✪☆☆☆☆☆☆

Target time: 3 minutes

Place a number in the middle box that divides into all the other numbers without leaving a remainder. The answer is greater than 1.

117		104
169		156
143		234

55 DIFFICULTY ⭐⭐⭐⭐☆☆☆☆☆☆

Target time: 6 minutes

Every row and column contains the same numbers and signs, but they are arranged in a different order each time. Find the correct order to arrive at the final totals shown.

7	x	4	−	2	+	5	=	31
							=	49
							=	13
							=	4
=		=		=		=		
8		10		23		16		

56 DIFFICULTY ✪✪✪✪✪✩✩✩✩✩
Target time: 6 minutes

Use one straight line to divide this circle into two sections, each with numbers adding up to the same total. Beware—all is not quite as it appears!

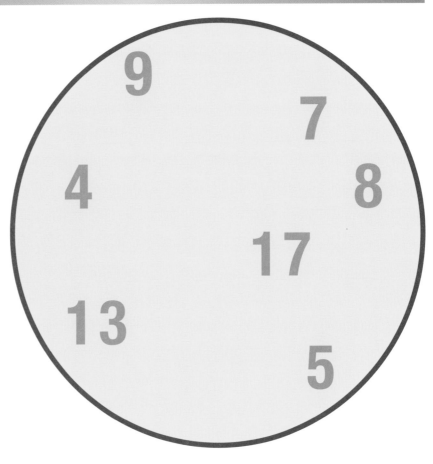

57 DIFFICULTY ✪✪✪✩✩✩✩✩✩✩
Target time: 2 minutes

What time should appear on the blank clock?

a

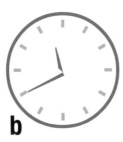

b

c

d

e

58 DIFFICULTY ✪✪✪✪✪✫✫✫✫✫
Target time: 3 minutes

Assess the cutlery below; given that scales a and b balance perfectly, how many knives are needed to balance scale c?

59 DIFFICULTY ★★★★★☆☆☆☆☆

Target time: 8 minutes

Find the answers to the calculations in the grid, looking up, down, backward, forward, and diagonally.

1. 888 + 888
2. 1,111 x 7
3. 21,402 ÷ 2
4. 33 x 333
5. 7 x 7 x 7 x 7
6. 303,030 ÷ 3
7. 1,110 x 9
8. 1,000 − 506
9. 3,434 ÷ 2
10. 101 x 72
11. 88,888 ÷ 2 ÷ 2
12. (2,133 ÷ 3) + 3 + 3

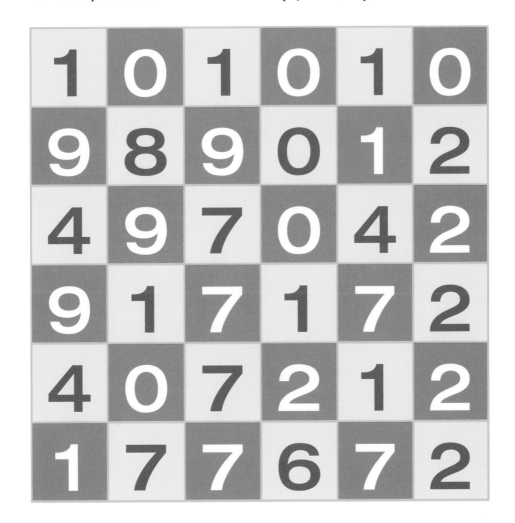

60 DIFFICULTY ✪✪✪✪✪✩✩✩✩✩
Target time: 8 minutes

Place the ace, king, queen, and jack of each suit so that:
* ★ no card value appears twice in any row, column, or main diagonal, and
* ★ no suit appears twice in any row, column, or main diagonal.

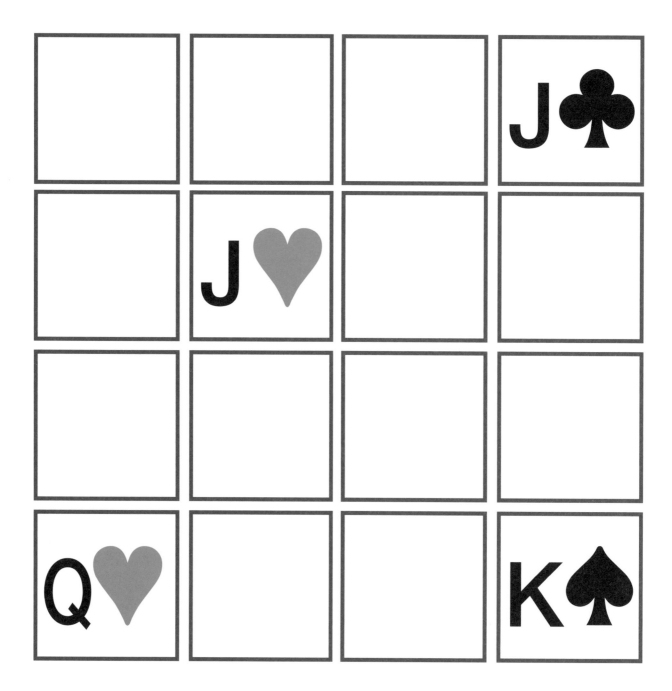

61 DIFFICULTY ●●●☆☆☆☆☆☆☆
Target time: 3 minutes

Make a calculation totaling the figure below using some or all of the numbers above it and any of the four standard mathematical operators (+, −, x, and ÷).

$$1 \quad 6 \quad 7 \quad 8 \quad 9 \quad 10$$

$$= 476$$

62 DIFFICULTY ●●●●☆☆☆☆☆☆
Target time: 4 minutes

Replace the question marks with mathematical symbols to produce the correct answer. Only the four basic operators (+, −, x, and ÷) are permitted. Perform calculations in strict left to right order. Can you find two possible solutions?

$$7 \; ? \; 6 \; ? \; 5 \; ? \; 4$$

$$= 2$$

This is a one-player solitaire game. Place two silver coins on spaces 1 and 2, and two pennies on spaces 9 and 10. The aim is to make the coins swap sides by sliding them along the lines.

However, there is a catch. At no point must a silver coin and a penny lie on the same line—for example, your opening move cannot be 2 to 4, because the silver coin at 4 and the penny at 9 would be on the same line. Also, only one coin per space is allowed.

How many moves are there in the shortest solution? One move counts as sliding one coin from one space along a straight line to another space, possibly moving through other spaces along the way, although if you wish to move the same coin along another line in a different direction, it counts as a second move.

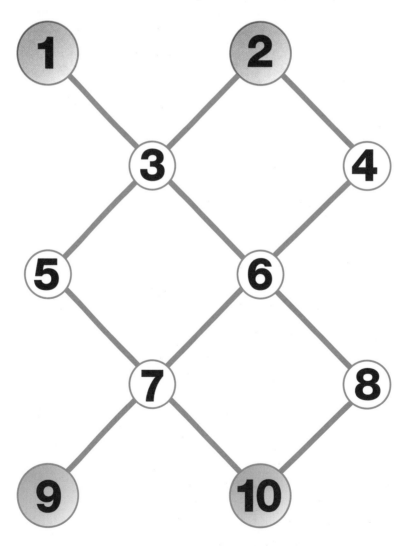

64 DIFFICULTY ✪✪✪✪✪✪✪☆☆
Target time: 5 minutes

Given that scales a and b balance perfectly, how many apples are needed to balance scale c?

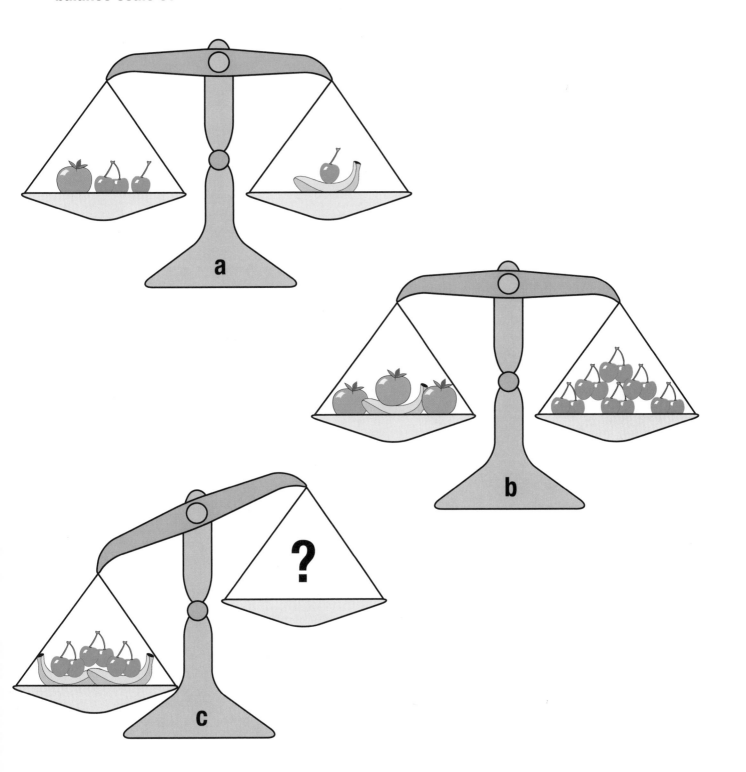

65 DIFFICULTY ★★★★★☆☆☆

Target time: 10 minutes

Can you fit these numbers into the grid? One number has already been inserted to help you get started.

3 Digits
323
669

4 Digits
2056
3212
5430
6742
7733
8060
8179
9055

5 Digits
14355
21845

28456
37206
37513
46207
49747
68626
75200
~~89505~~

6 Digits
317861
322009
479351
689083

7 Digits
1636986

2464093
3656016
3778443
4317723
4833109
5207007
5829464
6276067

6569248
7058756
8208754
8757623
9683726

66 DIFFICULTY ✪✪✪✪✪✪☆☆☆

Target time: 4 minutes

The number 1,970,157 appears just once in this grid and occurs in a straight line, running either backward or forward in a horizontal, vertical, or diagonal direction. Can you locate it?

1	9	5	1	9	7	0	9	7	5	9	1
9	7	1	7	9	5	0	1	5	7	9	9
5	0	0	9	0	9	9	0	1	1	9	1
0	9	7	5	9	7	7	9	7	0	7	7
9	5	1	9	1	5	1	0	0	5	0	0
7	9	7	0	5	7	9	9	1	7	9	9
1	1	5	7	0	1	1	0	0	5	1	5
7	7	0	9	9	5	7	0	7	9	1	7
0	0	1	5	9	9	9	5	9	1	7	1
5	7	0	0	1	0	1	7	0	9	5	7
9	9	7	0	5	9	0	7	1	5	7	0
1	1	5	9	1	7	5	9	0	7	9	1

67 DIFFICULTY ✪✪✪✪✪✪✪✪☆☆
Target time: 6 minutes

Which number comes next?

$2^3/_4$,　$13^3/_4$,　$5^1/_4$,

$9^1/_2$,　$7^3/_4$,　$5^1/_4$,　?

68 DIFFICULTY ✪✪✪✪☆☆☆☆☆☆
Target time: 4 minutes

Each block is equal to the sum of the two numbers beneath it.
Find all the missing numbers.

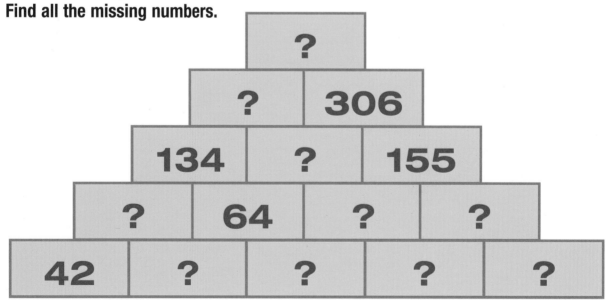

69 DIFFICULTY ✪✪✪✪✪✪☆☆☆☆
Target time: 3 minutes

Which is the odd number out?

3, 8, 15, 24, 29, 35, 48

70 DIFFICULTY ✪✪✪✪✪✪☆☆☆☆
Target time: 5 minutes

Adam and his sister Florence had a pair of standard dice and were playing a game where each needed to throw a double to start. On his very first turn, Adam threw a double six.

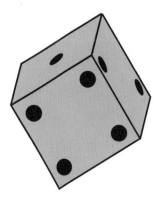

1. How likely was Florence to throw a double six on her next throw?

2. How likely was she to throw any double on her next throw?

3. What were the chances of Florence throwing, say, both a one and a six on her next throw?

4. How likely was she to throw her favorite number, four, on either of the die on her next throw?

71 DIFFICULTY ✪✪✪✪✪✪✪☆☆
Target time: 8 minutes

Place the ace, king, queen, and jack of each suit so that:
★ no card value appears twice in any row, column, or main diagonal, and
★ no suit appears twice in any row, column, or main diagonal.

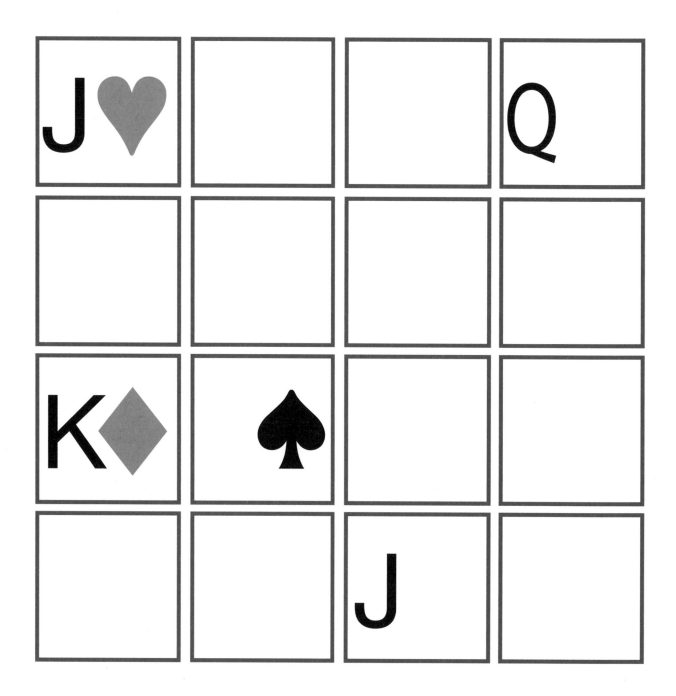

72 DIFFICULTY ✪✪✪✪✪✪✪✪☆☆
Target time: 8 minutes

Make a calculation totaling the figure below using some or all of the numbers above it and any of the four standard mathematical operators (+, −, x, and ÷).

2 4 6 7 8 9

= 628

73 DIFFICULTY ✪✪✪✪✪✪✪✪✪☆
Target time: 6 minutes

The cards on the right are valued as follows: an ace = 1, a jack = 11, a queen = 12, and a king = 13. All the other cards have the same value as their numbers.

Study this card arrangement carefully for one minute, then see if you can answer the questions on the next page without checking back.

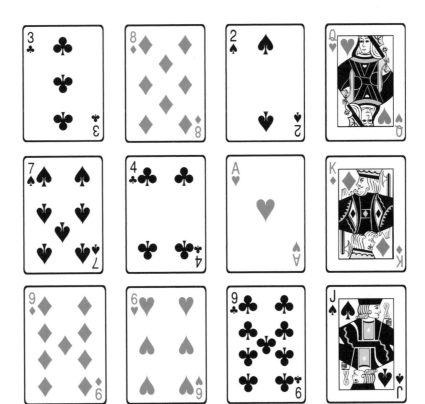

74 DIFFICULTY ✪✪✪✪✪✪✪☆☆
Target time: 6 minutes

Place a number in the middle box that divides into all the other numbers without leaving a remainder. The answer is greater than 1.

259		222
333		148
407		111

[73] DIFFICULTY ✪✪✪✪✪✪✪✪☆
Target time: 6 minutes

Can you answer these questions about the puzzle on the previous page without having to check back?

1. Which two numbers do not appear?

2. Which is the only pair of identical numbers to appear?

3. What is the highest total value of three cards in a column?

4. Two rows of four cards have the same total. What is this?

5. Which card is in the same column as (and directly below) a diamond, as well as being in the same column as (and directly above) a heart?

6. What is the total value of the four corner cards?

75 DIFFICULTY ✪✪✪✪✪✪✪☆☆
Target time: 10 minutes

Can you fit these numbers into the grid? One number has already been inserted to help you get started.

3 2 1 3 4

3 Digits
371
863

4 Digits
1756
2186
4096
5559
6058
7206
8282
9976

5 Digits
11654
24663
32134
33848
42676
58520

66750
72055
82518
94194

6 Digits
642001
704118
835656
861703

7 Digits
1429538
1704156
2138713
2752146
3458232
3495012
4805632
5819673
6157413

6720466
7137525
8561716
8744934
9357045

76 DIFFICULTY ✪✪✪✪✪✪✪✩✩
Target time: 5 minutes

Assess the symbols below. Given that scales a and b balance perfectly, how many spades are needed to balance scale c?

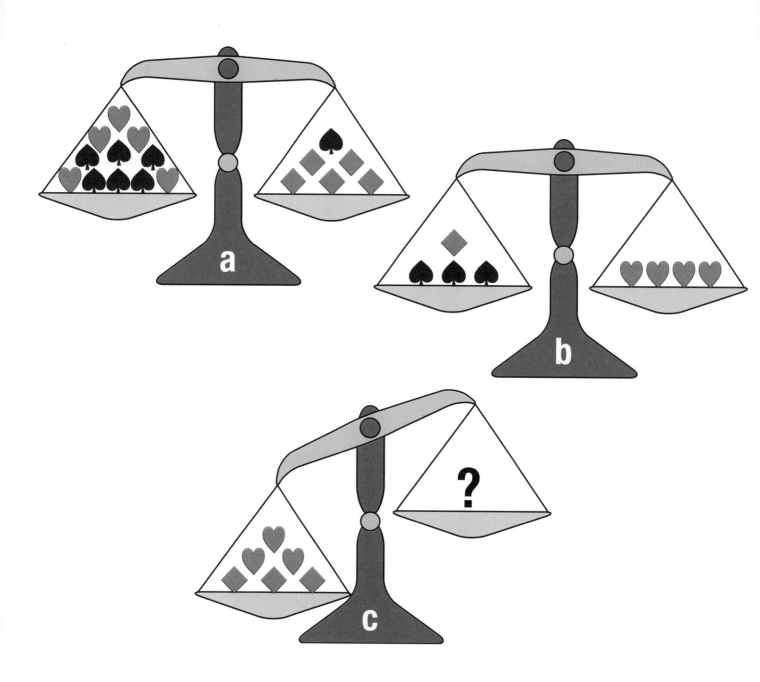

77 DIFFICULTY ✪✪✪✪✪✪✪☆☆

Target time: 5 minutes

Consider the celestial bodies below. Given that scales a and b balance perfectly, how many suns are needed to balance scale c?

78 DIFFICULTY ✪✪✪✪✪✩✩✩✩✩
Target time: 8 minutes

Find the answers to the following calculations in the grid below, reading up, down, backward, forward, and diagonally.

1. 10,000 − 5,454
2. 66 x 99
3. 4,224 x 2
4. 20,000 − 9,912
5. 52,000 ÷ 8
6. 5,555 − 4,321
7. 500 x 120
8. 1,604 x 5
9. 63,636 ÷ 3
10. (7 x 7) x (8 x 8)
11. 6,003 − 2,997
12. 101 x 10 x 9

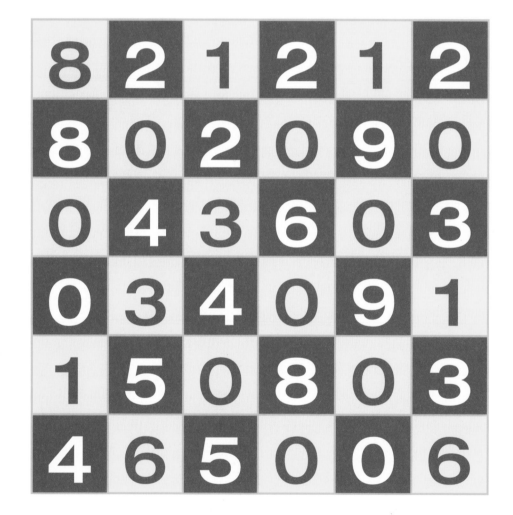

79 DIFFICULTY ★★★★☆☆☆☆☆☆
Target time: 3 minutes

Use two straight lines to divide this clock face into three parts, each containing numbers adding up to the same total.

80 DIFFICULTY ★★★★★★☆☆☆☆
Target time: 5 minutes

What number comes next in the sequence below?

-76, -27, -57, -46, -38, -65, ?

81 DIFFICULTY ✪✪✪✪✪✪☆☆☆☆
Target time: 6 minutes

Each block is equal to the sum of the two numbers beneath it.
Find all the missing numbers.

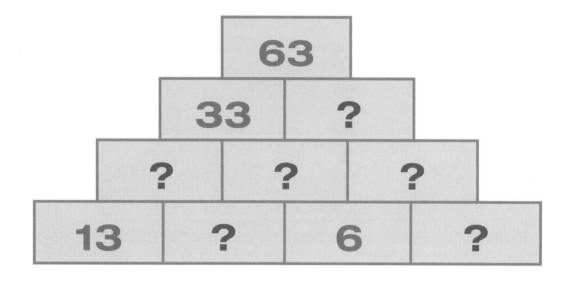

82 DIFFICULTY ✪✪✪✪✪✪☆☆☆☆
Target time: 3 minutes

Which number is the odd one out?

133, 171, 208, 247, 285

83 DIFFICULTY ✪✪✪✪✪✪☆☆☆☆
Target time: 7 minutes

Every row and column contains the same numbers and signs, but they are arranged in a different order each time. Find the correct order to arrive at the final totals shown.

20	+	5	–	11	x	6	=	84
							=	119
							=	125
							=	41
=		=		=		=		
75		95		69		65		

84 DIFFICULTY ★★★★★★☆☆☆☆
Target time: 6 minutes

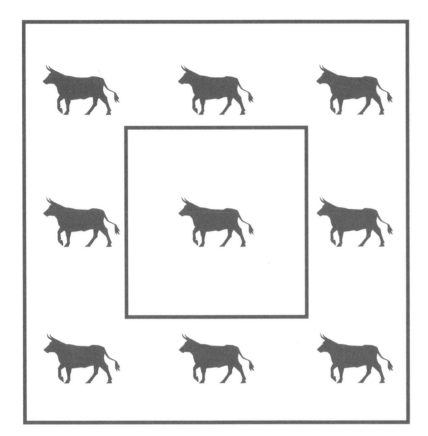

How many more square fences do you need to add so that each bull is separate from all the others?

85 DIFFICULTY ★★★★★★★★☆☆
Target time: 6 minutes

What number should replace the question mark in the following sequence?

365, 195, 380, 240, 395, 285, 410, ?

86 DIFFICULTY ✪✪✪✪✪✪✪☆☆☆
Target time: 20 minutes

Use skill (rather than luck) to solve this nonogram. (See puzzle 13 for advice on how to complete a nonogram.)

87 DIFFICULTY ✪✪✪✪✪☆☆☆☆☆
Target time: 3 minutes

What time should it be on clock f?

88 DIFFICULTY ✪✪✪✪☆☆☆☆☆☆
Target time: 4 minutes

Can you find either of the two possible solutions using any of the four standard mathematical operators (+, −, x, ÷)?

89 DIFFICULTY ✪✪✪✪✪✪✪☆☆
Target time: 8 minutes

Can you place the tiles in the grid so that:

* the odd numbers sit on the yellow spaces?
* the even numbers sit on the green spaces?
* each row, column, and main diagonal totals 34?

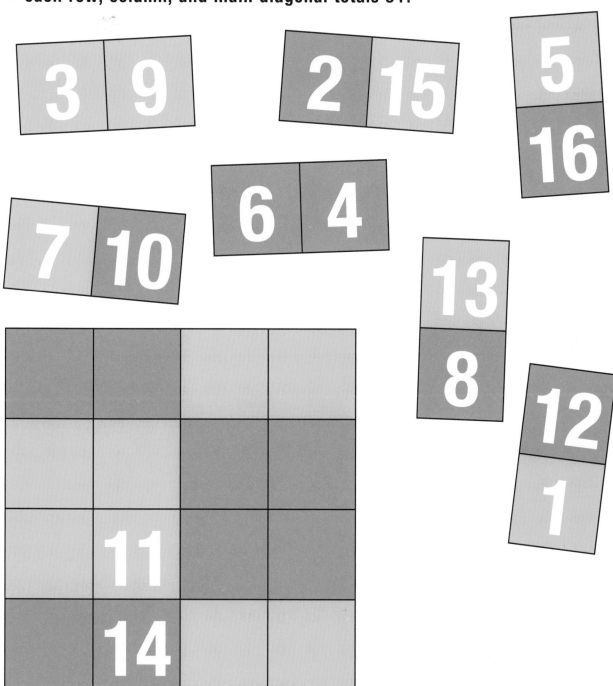

90 DIFFICULTY ✪✪✪✪✪✪✪✩✩✩
Target time: 10 minutes

Can you fit these numbers into the grid? One number has already been inserted to help you get started.

3 Digits
770
847

4 Digits
1805
2779
3586
4596
5358
6232
7519
8132

5 Digits
14385
23528
38923
46659
50658
61885
77576
82575
91513
92528

5 0 1 8 2 0 6

6 Digits	7 Digits	3199024	6714361
599560	1353745	4505979	7070873
784529	1379963	~~5018206~~	8171539
871625	2455298	5757336	9033244
934069	3129815	6208519	9726708

91 DIFFICULTY ✪✪✪✪✪✪✪✪☆☆
Target time: 10 minutes

The answers to the calculations below can be found in the grid—look up, down, backward, forward, and diagonally!

1. $(999 \div 3) \times 9^2$
2. $(2 + 2)^2 \times (3 + 3)^3$
3. 66×55
4. $(1{,}000{,}000 \div 50) \div 5$
5. $5{,}505.5 \times 2^4$
6. $(13{,}332 \times 2) \div 6$
7. $23 \times 24 \times 25$
8. $6{,}734 \times 3^2$
9. 101×11
10. 176×25
11. $(221 \div 13) + 1{,}717$
12. $163{,}216 \div 404$

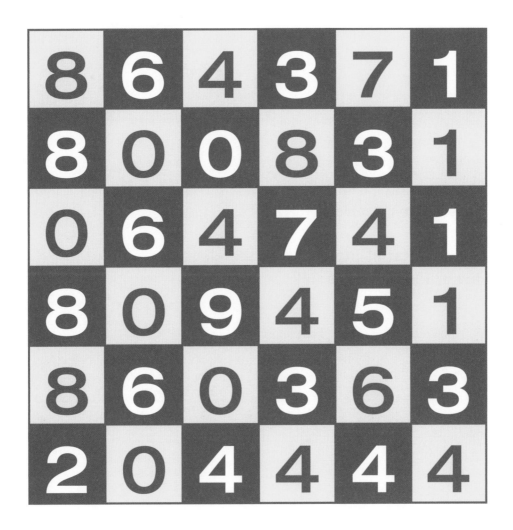

92 DIFFICULTY ✪✪✪✪✪✪✪✪☆☆

Target time: 6 minutes

How many squares on this miniature chess board can the knight visit (using his usual L-shaped move) without visiting a square twice?

93 DIFFICULTY ✪✪✪✪☆☆☆☆☆☆

Target time: 3 minutes

What is the sum total of the spots on the eleven hidden sides of these three dice?

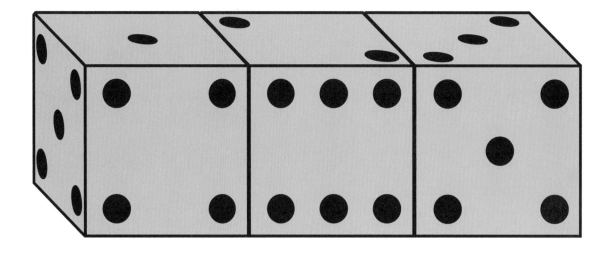

94 DIFFICULTY ✪✪✪✪✪✪✪✪☆☆
Target time: 6 minutes

Place a number in the middle box that divides into all the other numbers without leaving a remainder. The answer is greater than 1.

354

649

236

531

413

177

95 DIFFICULTY ✪✪✪✪✪✪☆☆☆☆
Target time: 3 minutes

Which number is the odd one out in this sequence?

7,246   7,326

7,270   7,393

7,297   7,359

96 DIFFICULTY ★★★★☆☆☆☆☆☆

Target time: 4 minutes

Replace the question marks with mathematical symbols to produce the correct answer. Only the four basic operators (+, −, x, and ÷) are permitted. Perform calculations in strict left to right order. Can you find all three possible solutions?

4 ? 3 ? 1 ? 2 = 9

97 DIFFICULTY ★★★★★☆☆☆☆☆

Target time: 4 minutes

Can you fit four different dominoes into the shape below, so that each horizontal and vertical line totals fourteen? We've placed two in their correct positions, although we haven't revealed how many dots (if any) should be on the second faces of these dominoes—you'll need to discover this, as well as the locations of the other dominoes, in order to arrive at the solution.

98 DIFFICULTY ✪✪✪✪✪✪☆☆☆☆

Target time: 7 minutes

The number 2,525,312 appears just once in this number-search grid and occurs in a straight line, running either backward or forward in a horizontal, vertical, or diagonal direction. Can you locate it?

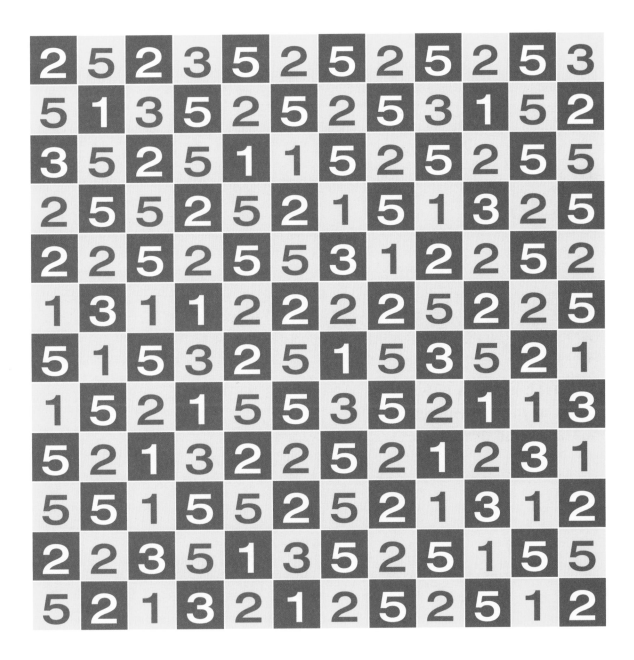

99 DIFFICULTY ✪✪✪✪✪✪✩✩✩✩
Target time: 6 minutes

Each block is equal to the sum of the two numbers beneath it. Find all the missing numbers.

		184		
	?		?	
?		?		113
24	13	?		?

100 DIFFICULTY ✪✪✪✪✪✪✪✩✩✩
Target time: 7 minutes

Again, each block is equal to the sum of the two numbers beneath it. Find them all.

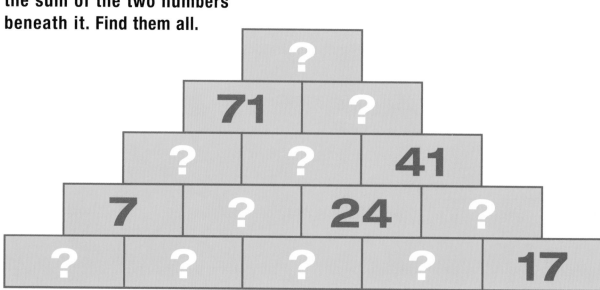

101 DIFFICULTY ✪✪✪✪✪✪✪☆☆☆
Target time: 10 minutes

Can you fit these numbers into the grid? One number has already been inserted to help you get started.

1 1 2 4 6

3 Digits
208
844

4 Digits
1067
2520
3148
4054
5329
7985
8982
9181

5 Digits
~~11246~~
20154
30171
43681
52734
53931
69418
73312
82362
92651

6 Digits
258231
623261
785984
993136

7 Digits
1064360

1911160
2031184
2296281
3822171
3893236
4411237
4636835
5150032

6659897
7221351
8603943
9296482
9546282

102 DIFFICULTY ✪✪✪✪✪✪✪✩✩
Target time: 6 minutes

Replace each star with a domino from the selection given below, so that the sum of every set of four connected by a black line is the same. One domino is already in position as a starter.

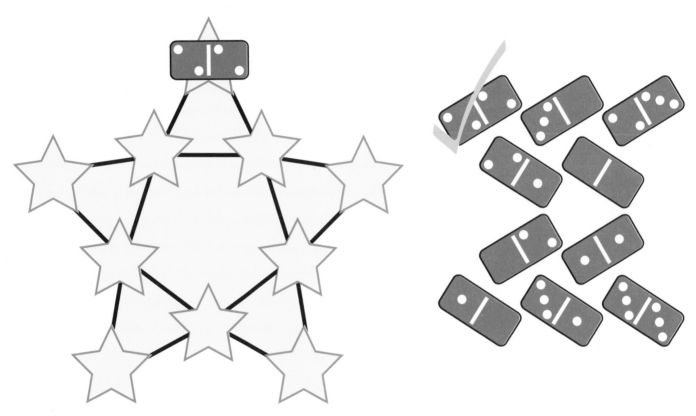

103 DIFFICULTY ✪✪✪✪✪✪✩✩✩✩
Target time: 5 minutes

What number should replace the question mark in the following sequence?

2,468, 8,652, 2,668, 8,672, ?

104 DIFFICULTY ✪✪✪✪✪✪✪✪☆☆
Target time: 10 minutes

The answers to the following calculations are embedded in the grid below—look up, down, backward, forward, and diagonally!

1. 24 x 365
2. 60 x 24 x 7
3. 60 x 60 x 24
4. 123,456 ÷ 3
5. (7 x 6 x 5) x (4 x 3 x 2)
6. (565 ÷ 5) x 13

7. 17.5% x 50,000
8. (888 ÷ 4) x 44
9. 10^2 x 9^2
10. 13,578 − 6,789
11. 198,198 ÷ 99

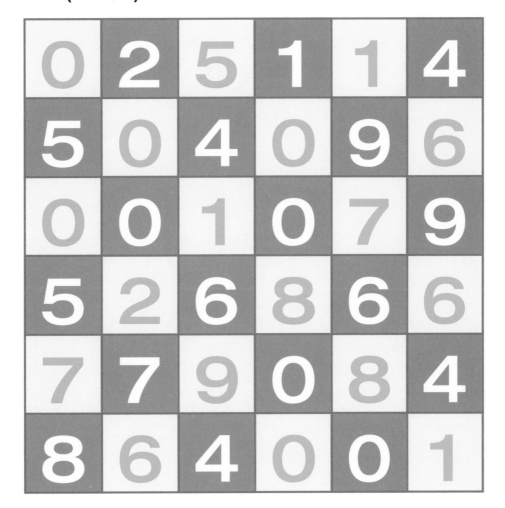

105 DIFFICULTY ✪✪✪✪✪✪☆☆☆☆
Target time: 6 minutes

What time should it be on clock f?

106 DIFFICULTY ✪✪✪✪✪✪☆☆☆☆
Target time: 6 minutes

Use three straight lines to divide this shape into four equally shaped sections, each containing three numbers adding up to the same total.

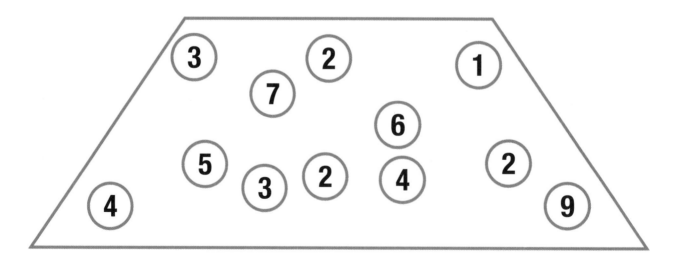

107 DIFFICULTY ✪✪✪✪✪✪✪✪☆

Target time: 6 minutes

2,166, 644, 1,255, 273, 819, 3,437, 5,128

Which is the odd number out?

108 DIFFICULTY ✪✪✪✪✪✪✪☆☆

Target time: 5 minutes

Juliette has lined up these three dice on her coffee table. She can see the same seven faces that you can see, and Angelica (her friend, sitting opposite) can see the top three faces of the dice, as well as a further four faces you and Juliette cannot see. None of you can see the bottom three faces of these dice. What is the total number of spots on all the faces of the dice that Angelica can see, given that this is a higher number than the total number of spots you can see?

109 DIFFICULTY ✪✪✪✪✪✪✪✪☆☆
Target time: 6 minutes

Place a number in the middle box that divides into all the other numbers without leaving a remainder. The answer is greater than 1.

141		517
376		611
564		423

110 DIFFICULTY ✪✪✪✪✪✪☆☆☆☆
Target time: 4 minutes

Moving east or south all the time, how many routes go from a to b that pass through one star at most?

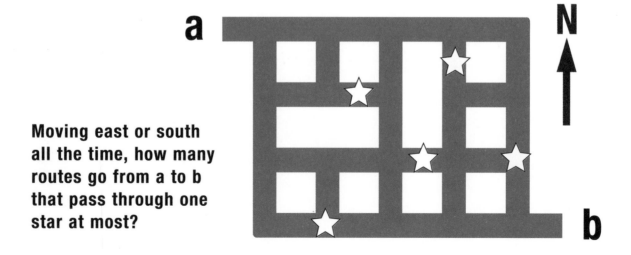

111 DIFFICULTY ★★★★★★☆☆☆☆

Target time: 7 minutes

Every row and column contains the same numbers and signs, but they are arranged in a different order each time. Find the correct order to arrive at the final totals shown.

15	–	4	x	9	+	14	=	113
	■		■		■		■	
							=	225
	■		■		■		■	
							=	137
	■		■		■			■
							=	35
=	■	=	■	=	■	=	■	
257		55		89		77		

112 DIFFICULTY ★★★★★★☆☆☆☆
Target time: 6 minutes

Each block is equal to the sum of the two numbers beneath. Find all the missing numbers (clue: Some contain fractions).

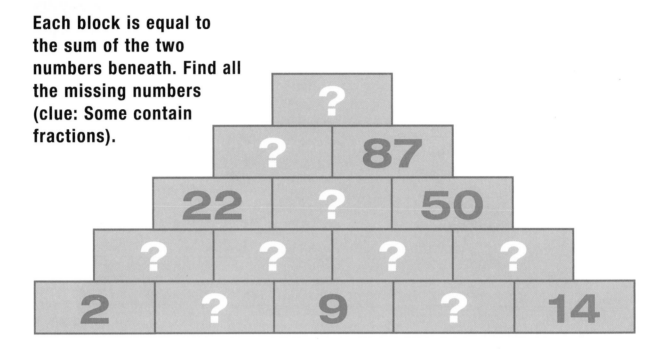

113 DIFFICULTY ★★★★★★★★☆☆
Target time: 6 minutes

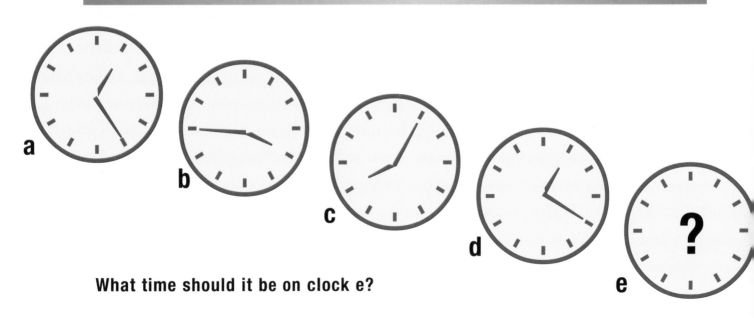

What time should it be on clock e?

114 DIFFICULTY ✪✪✪✪✪✪✪☆☆
Target time: 8 minutes

Can you place the tiles in the grid so that:
* there is one square of every color in every row and column, and
* every row, column, and main diagonal totals 34?

	3		2
		5	
1		4	

14

15   16

6   7   9

10   11   8   13

            12

115 DIFFICULTY ✪✪✪✪✪✪✰✰✰

Target time: 5 minutes

Can you find both of the possible solutions using any of the four standard mathematical operators (+, −, x, ÷)?

5 ? 19 ? 6

? 1 = 4

116 DIFFICULTY ✪✪✪✪✪✪✪✪✪✰

Target time: 6 minutes

Don't be alarmed! Study these clock radios carefully for ninty seconds, noting the station to which they are tuned, the actual time, and the time the alarm is due to go off, then see if you can answer the questions on page 216 without checking back.

Music 197
6:35 P.M.
🔔 6:35 A.M.

News 350
11:15 P.M.
🔔 5:55 A.M.

Sports 1532
12:25 A.M.
🔔 7:15 A.M.

Talk 820
10:40 P.M.
🔔 8:20 A.M.

117 DIFFICULTY ✪✪✪✪✪✪✪☆☆☆
Target time: 10 minutes

Can you fit these numbers into the grid? One number has already been inserted to help you get started.

8 3 7 2 9

3 Digits
513
885

4 Digits
2812
3916
4854
5194
6902
7044
8638
9658

5 Digits
10681
22799
31668
43413
52842
63207
68529
71334
~~83729~~
94096

6 Digits
198953
219069
787265
883473

7 Digits
1166871

1431596
2378257
2541503
3130442
4411455
5298198
6032926
6351914

7617621
7651341
8265257
9133382
9715944

118 DIFFICULTY ⊕⊕⊕⊕⊕⊕☆☆☆☆
Target time: 5 minutes

Make a calculation totaling the figure on the right using some or all of the numbers below with any of the four standard mathematical operators (+, −, x, and ÷).

$$4 \quad 4 \quad 5 \quad 5 \quad 7 \quad 7 = 900$$

[116] DIFFICULTY ⊕⊕⊕⊕⊕⊕⊕⊕⊕☆
Target time: 6 minutes

Can you answer these questions about puzzle 116 without checking back?

1. The alarm on which color of clock radio is scheduled to go off at the latest time?

2. What station is tuned in on the clock radio with an alarm scheduled to go off exactly twelve hours later than its current time?

3. What is the current time on the station tuned to News 350?

4. What station is the sports channel?

5. Assuming each of the owners of the four pictured clock radios will fall asleep at exactly their clock's current time and will wake as soon as their alarm sounds, what station will the person who will have the least sleep be listening to when their alarm goes off?

6. What color is the clock radio that is tuned in to a channel that has the same number as the time of its alarm?

119 DIFFICULTY ✪✪✪✪✪✪✪☆☆
Target time: 5 minutes

Given that scales a and b balance perfectly, how many circles are needed to balance scale c?

120 DIFFICULTY ✪✪✪✪✪✪✪☆☆☆
Target time: 5 minutes

Which is the odd one out?

4,396 4,250 7,586

9,237 4,805 9,782

121 DIFFICULTY ✪✪✪✪✪✪✪☆☆☆
Target time: 10 minutes

The square below contains exactly one of each of the thirty-six faces from six standard dice. In each horizontal row of six smaller squares and each vertical column of six smaller squares, there are faces with different numbers of spots. There is no face with five spots in either of the two long diagonal lines of six smaller squares. The total number of spots in the diagonal line from top left to bottom right is seventeen, and that in the diagonal line from top right to bottom left is twenty-three. We've placed a few to give you a start, but can you place the rest?

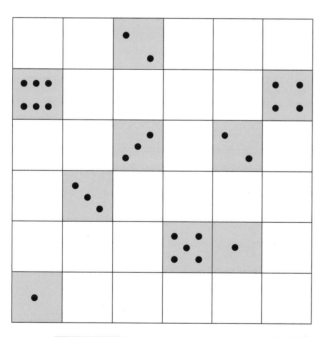

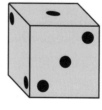

122 DIFFICULTY ✪✪✪✪✪✪✪✩✩

Target time: 10 minutes

The answers to the following calculations can be found in the grid—look up, down, backward, forward, and diagonally!

1. 22 x 33 x 44
2. (123 + 123) x 123
3. (989 − 323) x 6
4. (2 + 3) x (4 + 5) x (6 + 7) x (8 + 9)
5. (9^2) x (5^2)
6. 76,544 + 123,456
7. 30,800 ÷ 7
8. 5.5 x 666
9. (111 x 3 x 3) + 2
10. 12,250 ÷ 35
11. 10^3 + 10
12. 9,494 ÷ 2

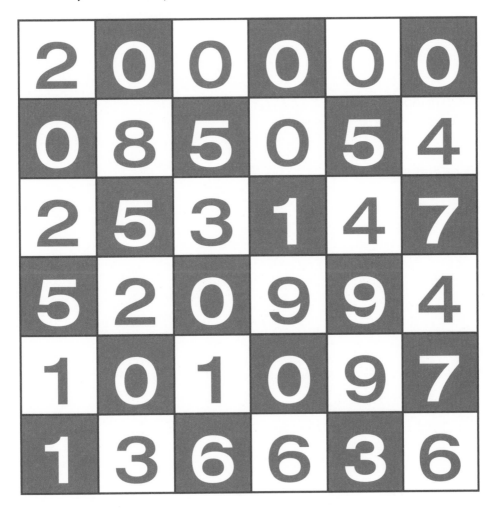

2	0	0	0	0	0
0	8	5	0	5	4
2	5	3	1	4	7
5	2	0	9	9	4
1	0	1	0	9	7
1	3	6	6	3	6

123 DIFFICULTY ✪✪✪✪✪✪✪☆☆
Target time: 6 minutes

What is the smallest number of coins that need to be moved so that the coins inside one box total exactly twice the value of those in the other? Think laterally for this one!

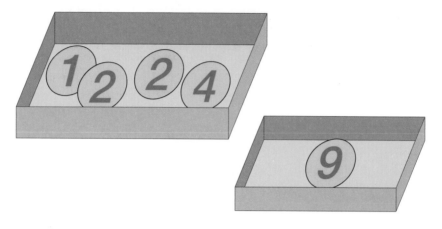

124 DIFFICULTY ✪✪✪✪✪✪☆☆☆☆
Target time: 5 minutes

Which number comes next?

1,447, 1,491, 1,540, 1,594, 1,653, ?

125 DIFFICULTY ✪✪✪✪✪✪✩✩✩✩
Target time: 4 minutes

What time should it be on clock e?

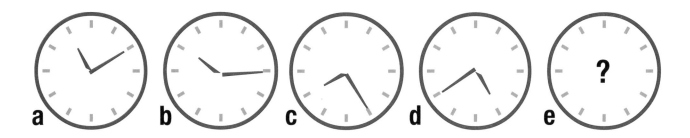

a   b   c   d   e

126 DIFFICULTY ✪✪✪✪✪✪✪✪✪✪
Target time: 8 minutes

Replace the question marks with mathematical symbols to produce the correct answer. Only the four basic operators (+, –, x, and ÷) are permitted. Perform calculations in strict left to right order. Can you find two possible solutions?

$$5 \; ? \; \tfrac{1}{2} \; ? \; \tfrac{1}{4} \; ? \; 6 = 8\tfrac{1}{4}$$

127 DIFFICULTY ✪✪✪✪✪✪✪✪✩✩
Target time: 8 minutes

Can you place the tiles in the grid so that:
* the colors form a checkerboard pattern, and
* each row, column, and main diagonal totals the same number?
Note: Look at the tiles from all angles!

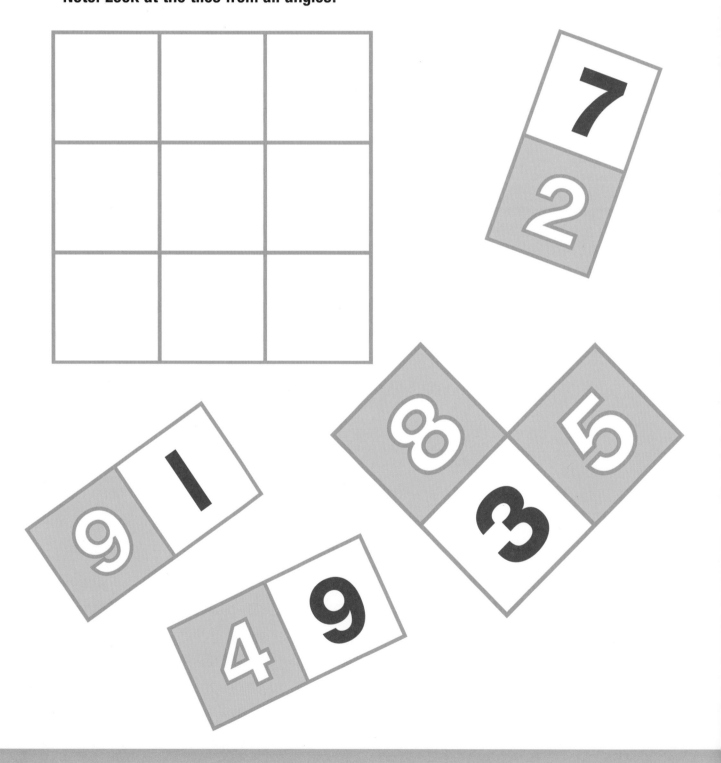

128 DIFFICULTY ✪✪✪✪✪✪✪✰✰
Target time: 8 minutes

Each block is equal to the sum of the two numbers beneath it. Find all the missing numbers.

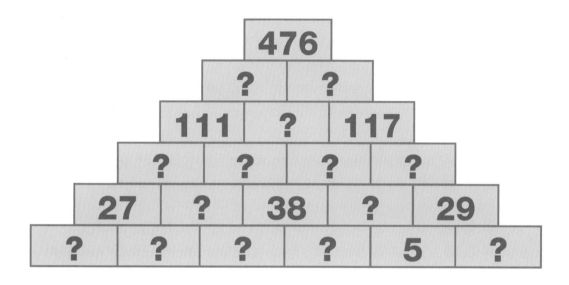

129 DIFFICULTY ✪✪✪✪✪✪✰✰✰✰
Target time: 5 minutes

Which number comes next?

34, 77, 154, 605, 1,111, ?

130 DIFFICULTY ✪✪✪✪✪✪☆☆☆☆
Target time: 5 minutes

Which number should take the place of the question mark?

18

6

2

?

131 DIFFICULTY ✪✪✪✪✪✪✪✪☆☆
Target time: 6 minutes

Using a standard set of dominoes (as pictured here), start with the double blank and form a continuous snake by joining all but one of the dominoes end to end until you reach the double six. Dominoes must be joined according to the normal rules of the game, i.e., the adjacent sides of touching dominoes must always be the same. This can be achieved in many ways, but only if one domino is discarded. So which one is the domi-"no-no"?

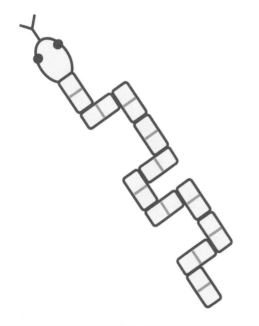

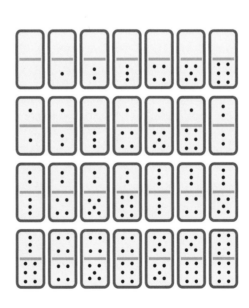

132 DIFFICULTY ✪✪✪✪✪✪✪✪☆☆
Target time: 5 minutes

Place a number in the middle box that divides into all the other numbers without leaving a remainder. The answer is greater than 1.

882		441
504		567
693		315

133 DIFFICULTY ✪✪✪✪✪✪✪✪✪✪
Target time: 10 minutes

Without lifting pencil from paper, draw straight lines to divide this heart into six parts, each containing four different numbers.

134 DIFFICULTY ✪✪✪✪✪✪✪✪✪✩
Target time: 6 minutes

What number should replace the question mark in the following sequence?

23, 28, 43, 65, 98, ?

135 DIFFICULTY ✪✪✪✪✪✪✩✩✩✩
Target time: 4 minutes

Where should the minute hand point on clock e?

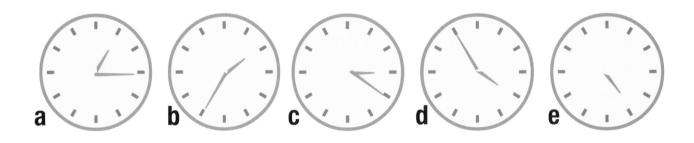

a   b   c   d   e

136 DIFFICULTY ✪✪✪✪✪✪✪✪✪✪

Target time: 8 minutes

Each block is equal to the sum of the two numbers beneath it.
Find all the missing numbers.

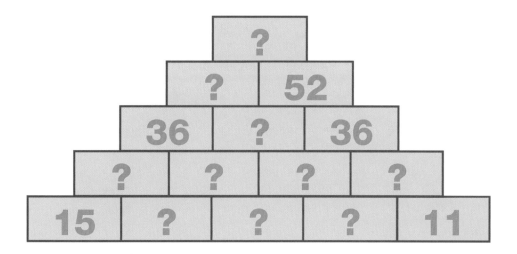

137 DIFFICULTY ✪✪✪✪✪✪✩✩✩✩

Target time: 3 minutes

Which number is the odd one out?

15, 24, 35, 48, 64, 80

138 DIFFICULTY ✪✪✪✪✪✪☆☆☆
Target time: 20 minutes

A right royal nonogram for all you cardsharks. (See puzzle 13 for advice on how to complete a nonogram.)

Column clues (top):

```
                                        2 1 2 1
                    1                   1 1 1 1 2 1         1
                    2     2     1 2       2 1 1 2 2 5 1 1 2     2 2
4                   1 2 1   1 12 1 3    15 1 2 1 1 2 1 2 1     2 5 1 1 6
1                   4 1 2 17 2 2 1 14 1 1 2 1 3 1 2 1 1 2     1 5 1 4 1
1         10        1 1 2 2 2 3 2 2 1 2 1 1 1 1 1 1 3 3 16 1 4 2 1 1 5
1       1 7         1 2 2 2 2 2 2 2 1 2 2 4 6 1 2 3 5 3 3 5 1 4 2 1 3 8
2 13 1 6 1 8 2 3 1 1 1 2 3 1 2 3 1 7 1 7 1 1 4 7 1 2 1 1 3 4
```

Row clues (left):

```
                              2 1
2 1 1 1 1 1 1 1             1 2
                          2 1 13
                          5 1
                          1 11
                          7 2
              1 1 1 1     1 1
              1 1 1 5 4   1
              1 1 1 2 3   4
            1 1 1 1 1 1   1
            1 1 1 1 1 1   1
            1 1 1 1 1 1   1
          1 1 1 1 1 3 1   1
        4 1 1 1 2 1 1     1
        2 1 1 1 1 3 2     2
      2 1 1 1 1 1 1 1     1
      8 1 1 1 2 1 1 2     2
        4 2 1 2 1 1 1     8
        5 2 1 1 1 4 2     4
      6 2 1 1 1 1 1 2     4
          7 2 2 1 2 3     5
      3 1 3 2 1 1 1 4     1
          3 1 2 2 2 3     6
              7 2 10 3    2
              3 17 2      4
        2 1 1 2 1 3 2 1   1
  1 1 2 1 1 2 1 3 1       3
        8 1 1 1 3 1 4     2
      2 1 2 1 1 1 1 2     4
        1 2 1 2 1 6 3     1
```

139 DIFFICULTY ★★★★★★☆☆☆☆
Target time: 5 minutes

Make a calculation totaling the figure below, using some or all of the numbers above it with any of the four standard mathematical operators (+, −, x, and ÷).

4 7 9 10 25 75

= 924

140 DIFFICULTY ★★★★☆☆☆☆☆☆
Target time: 4 minutes

These dominoes follow a certain
sequence, so can you tell what should
be in the empty space?

 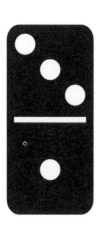   

141 DIFFICULTY ✪✪✪✪✪✪✪✪✪✰
Target time: 6 minutes

Which is the odd number out?

5,431   5,437

5,449   5,464

5,471   5,477

142 DIFFICULTY ✪✪✪✪✪✪✪✪✪✪
Target time: 7 minutes

What number should replace the question mark in the following sequence?

75,634, 48,192, ?, 7,320, 1,460

143 DIFFICULTY ✪✪✪✪✪✪✪✪☆☆
Target time: 10 minutes

The answers to the calculations below can be found in the grid—look up, down, backward, forward, and diagonally!

1. (2 x 3 x 4) x (5 x 6 x 7)
2. 123 x 321
3. 2 x 22 x 222
4. 5,656 + 7,878
5. 220^2
6. 10,000 – 6,666 – 666 – 66 – 6
7. (99 – 2) x (99 + 2)
8. 71,104 ÷ 8
9. (26,400 ÷ 2) ÷ 3
10. (747 x 5) x 2
11. 14^4

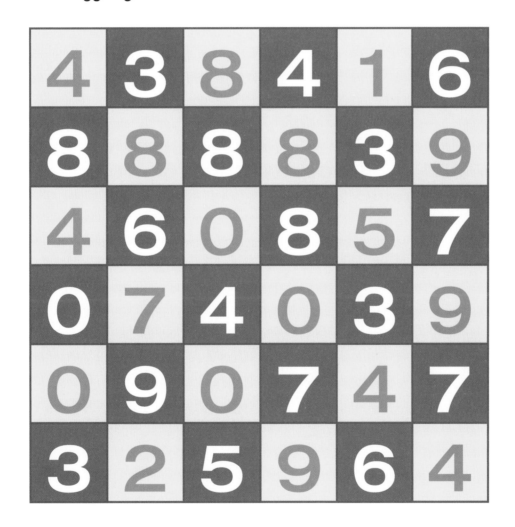

144 DIFFICULTY ✪✪✪✪✪✪✪✩✩

Target time: 7 minutes

Replace the question marks with mathematical symbols to produce the correct answer. Only the four basic operators (+, −, x, and ÷) are permitted. Perform calculations in strict left to right order. Can you find all three possible solutions?

24 ? 6 ? 9 ? 2

=18

145 DIFFICULTY ✪✪✪✪✪✪✪✪✪✪

Target time: 6 minutes

When these four tiles are arranged correctly, the pattern shown is a continuous loop. What is the least number of 90-degree revolutions needed to achieve this. Some lateral thinking may be necessary!

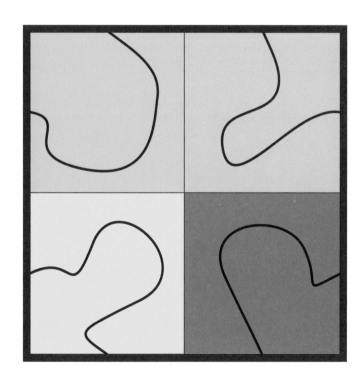

146 DIFFICULTY ✪✪✪✪✪✪✪☆☆
Target time: 8 minutes

Can you place the tiles in the grid so that:
* each row and column contains three squares of each color, and
* each row and column contains exactly one of each number?

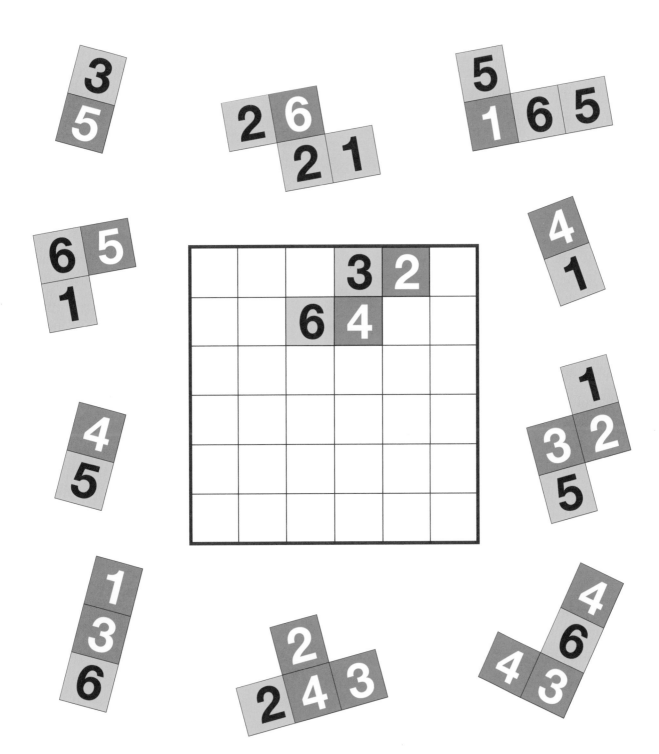

ANSWERS

1

1	2	3	4
4	1	2	3
2	3	4	1
3	4	1	2

2

```
1 0 7 4 3   7 8 7 4 1 8
8 1 1   1   5   3   2   7
7   9 4 7 4 2   4 6 9 8 3 8 2
4   3   3   9   1   0   6   7
6 5 7 8   3 4 7 4 9   2 4 6 6
4   8   7   9   4   8   5   2
4 6 8 7 3 3 3   2 4 0 2 3 2 6
          8           7
6 4 8 0 1 8 3   5 3 5 9 6 8 1
1   9   1   2   6   3   7   1
6 3 1 6   1 4 9 2 0   1 3 0 5
2   4   3   1   1   5   4   8
3 1 9 3 2 1 0   5 1 3 4 9   0
    1   6   9   9   9   6 9 0
  4 3 2 8 3 6   9 2 6 0 7
```

3

(25 x 5 x 4) + (9 x 3) = 527
There are ten other
possible solutions.

4

1. 19
2. 1 + 2 + 3 = 6
3. 7
4. Green
5. 2 (1 and 3)
6. 9
7. 4
8. 2

5

b; the other three have
the same angle between
the hands.

6

Follow the route marked
by the red squares:
(3 x 5 + 3 ÷ 6 + 2 − 1 = 4)

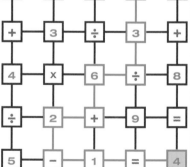

7

Three; each apple weighs as much as two oranges, and each banana weighs as much as four oranges. Thus three apples are needed to balance scale c.

8

1. 6,561
2. 2,000
3. 1,232
4. 10,100
5. 352
6. 6,170
7. 2,904
8. 1,000
9. 7,654
10. 1,782
11. 520
12. 30,330
13. 2,260

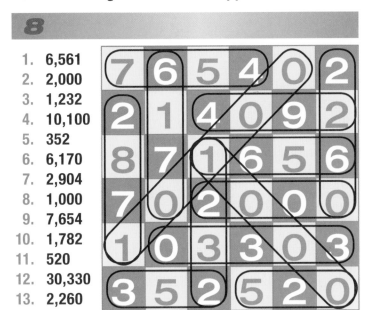

9

3	+	2	x	6	−	5	=	25
x		x				−		
6	−	3	x	5	+	2	=	17
+		+		+		x		
5	+	6	−	2	x	3	=	27
−		−		x		+		
2	+	5	−	3	x	6	=	24
=		=		=		=		
21		7		9		15		

10

Remove one coin from the bottom row to leave five coins remaining. The crux of the problem is the single coin in the top row, and uses logic of odd and even numbers. If your opponent takes it at any stage, make sure your next move leaves the two larger rows equal in coins. Until that happens, ensure that the two larger rows are one coin different (e.g., 2 and 3).

11

```
5 4 3 7 9 8 7 3 5 4 9 5
9 8 3 5 9 3 7 5 3 4 8 4
3 4 7 5 4 3 5 9 5 3 7 7
4 5 4 9 4 5 8 4 7 3 9 3
5 4 3 7 9 3 3 8 5 9 8 8
9 3 4 8 5 7 9 9 4 9 9 9
4 7 9 4 9 8 9 7 7 3 4 5
8 5 9 5 4 3 5 8 9 8 8 3
7 9 5 3 5 [9 8 7 3 4 5] 9
5 1 4 7 4 8 7 5 9 7 5 3
8 5 3 5 3 3 4 9 5 8 4 4
9 8 7 3 5 4 5 4 3 9 7 8
```

12

```
7 6 1 5 4       9 4 2 8 2 9
8 7 7     8   9   4     5   5
2     7 3 2 1 4   6 4 9 8 8 7 7
8   6   1   8   1   4   6     1
7 2 6 3     2 0 9 0 1     2 6 8 0
3   7   3   8   3   5   4     4
6 0 2 9 2 5 7   1 4 1 9 6 9 4
          8             2
7 4 7 2 5 1 7   6 8 1 7 5 1 1
5   9   0   6   0   5   6     1
1 5 7 2     2 4 4 4 3     7 4 2 5
5   2   2   7   8   9   5     6
9 8 7 7 6 8   9 7 4 9 2       9
    3   5   8   3   8   3 1 5
7 3 9 7 1 5   3 0 4 0 5
```

13

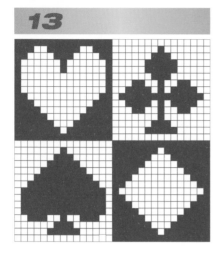

14

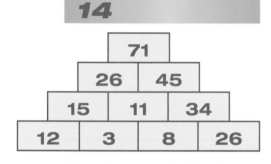

15

b is at (9, 6) and d is at (5, 0). The secret is to work out that the average of a and c's coordinates give the center of the square as (7, 3).

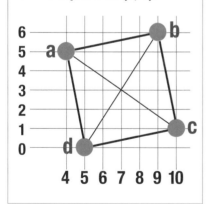

16

486; all the others have their digits in ascending order.

17

((6 ÷ 2) x 3) + 7 = 16;   (6 x 2) − 3 + 7 = 16

18

5	4	3	1
2	1	4	3
4	3	1	5
3	2	5	4

19

20

21

Gary won $4. The total payback is three times the difference of the number of spots on the two dice. Thus Gary got back $9: (5 − 2) x 3 = 9, winning $4.

21

Ten; from b we can infer that three moons equals one star; from a we can thus infer that seven moons equals five suns. If we then convert the left-hand side of c into moons we get fourteen moons (because each star is worth three moons). As we know that seven moons equals five suns, we can deduce that twice that will need ten suns to balance scale c.

22

91.25; deduct 1.25, then 2.5 alternately.

23

80; write the points as digits, then add them up in rows:

a.   13 + 21 = 34
b.   40 + 11 = 51
c.   26 + 45 = 71
so d. 45 + 35 = 80

24

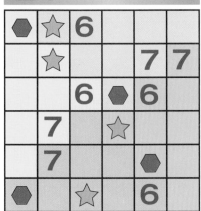

25

26

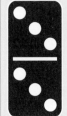

a; the dots in the upper part of each domino increase in number by one every time, while those in the lower part decrease by one every time, thus the total number of dots on each domino remains the same every time.

27

17

28

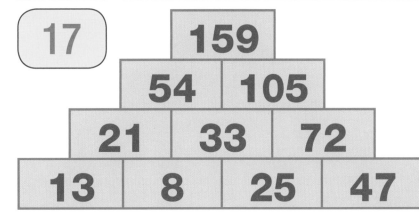

29

4,569; in all the others the third digit is the sum of the first two digits, and the fourth digit is the sum of the second and third digits.

30

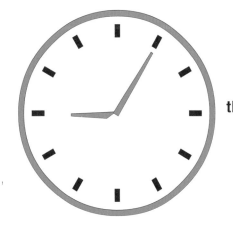

9:05 (add 35 minutes, then 30, then 25...)

31

12 − 4 + 7 − 8 = 7
((12 − 4) x 7) ÷ 8 = 7

32

```
  8 1 5 8 7   9 1 6 1 1 5
6 7 5   3   8   2   9   7
8   8 7 4 4 9   6 0 1 5 1 1 7
1   9   3   5   4   1   2   4
2 5 3 4   4 6 2 5 5   7 4 0 3
0   3   2   1   3   3   7   6
2 0 4 1 0 1 9   3 7 5 6 0 7 6
          0           0
5 1 7 9 1 5 3   4 5 4 9 4 2 8
7   8   0   4   1   1   0   1
4 8 1 2   6 9 6 0 6   4 9 8 3
8   0   9   6   9   3   9   0
8 1 0 7 4 0 8   5 7 1 9 3   2
      6   6   8   0   4   5 4 4
  3 7 9 2 5 3   9 2 5 7 9
```

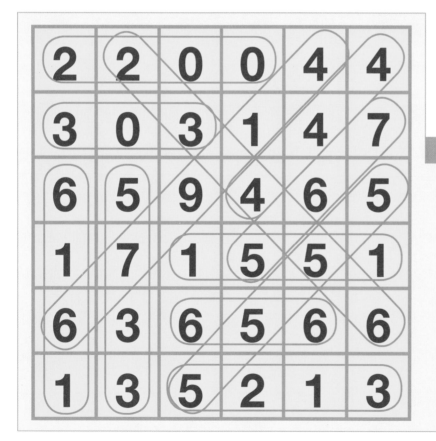

33

Fourteen; one spade weighs as much as four clubs, and one heart weighs as much as six clubs. Thus fourteen clubs are needed to balance scale c.

34

42; all of the others are prime numbers.

35

Gary won $8. The total payback is the number of points on the first die multiplied by the number of points on the second. Thus Gary got back $20 (5 x 4 = 20), winning $8.

36

1. 41,976
2. 3,375
3. 1,616
4. 2,200
5. 23,456
6. 303
7. 1,551
8. 5,555
9. 444
10. 3,125
11. 765
12. 656

37

1. 2; the triangle (7) and pentagon (23)
2. 16 + 7 = 23
3. 4 x 16 = 64
4. Triangle (7) and pentagon (23)
5. Pink (16), blue (4), and lilac (46)
6. 35; 7 + 4 = 11, 46 − 11 = 35

38

The Pythagorean Theorem. Consider Fig. 1. The length of this square's sides is the same as the hypotenuse (longest side) of any of the triangles. In Fig. 2, we have rearranged the same shapes into a different configuration, so the areas must be equal. There are two squares (separated by the dotted line). The left-hand square has sides equivalent to the middle-length side of the triangle, while the sides of the right-hand square are equal to the triangle's shortest side. In other words, the square of the hypotenuse is equal to the sum of the squares of the other two sides, which is the Pythagorean Theorem.

39

$(((7 \times 4) + 4) \times 10) − 9 = 311$. There are thirteen other possible solutions.

40

```
1 8 0 4 8 7 0 9 1 8 0 4
4 7 8 0 9 8 1 9 9 8 1 0
4 1 0 0 7 9 8 9 1 7 4 0
7 8 9 0 1 4 7 0 9 1 9 8
4 9 0 4 7 8 4 8 1 0 7 7
8 9 8 7 0 9 0 8 9 0 0 9
9 0 7 9 4 8 9 1 4 9 0 4
8 8 4 9 8 1 9 4 9 7 8 9
1 0 7 8 4 9 0 1 8 9 4 9
9 7 9 1 4 0 1 8 0 9 8 0
4 9 8 0 8 4 0 8 1 4 7 8
8 7 1 1 4 1 9 8 7 9 1 1
```

41

				3	3		
		1					
		1			2		1
				4	4	2	
2	2						3
	4						3
	4						

42

(dominoes)

43

11

44

846; it should be 847 since each number is reversed then added on to the previous number.

45

Follow the route marked in green.

66	14	18	65	26	55	19
77	50	21	16	49	24	63
75	33	37	78	40	54	10
96	98	96	25	18	15	36
31	20	36	49	54	50	56
98	48	11	23	91	72	56
20	28	45	78	91	15	72
12	23	54	77	85	95	21
16	25	24	66	14	91	40

46

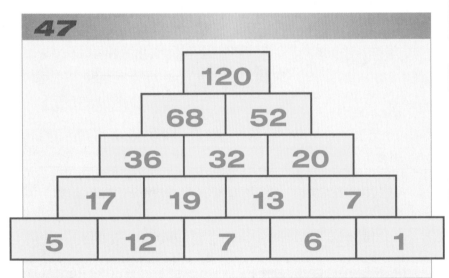

47

		120		
	68		52	
	36	32	20	
17	19	13	7	
5	12	7	6	1

48

14; there are two sequences running alternately.
Starting with 10, add 2, 4, 6, etc.
Starting with 5, add 1, 3, 5, etc.
So 9 + 5 = 14.

49

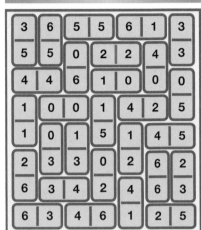

50

			3	1			
3	5					4	5
	1		2	4		2	
			3		1		
5					4		4
	2	3		5		1	
						2	

51

((6 x 2) − 4) ÷ 2 = 4
((3 + 5) x 3) ÷ 4 = 6
(5 + 2 − 3) ÷ 2 = 2

52

9,461; the rest can be
paired off into anagrams
of one another:
2,743–3,724; 9,172–
2,917; 6,813–1,836;
4,819–9,418.

53

3; because the big circle centered around that number encompasses three of the other numbers (1, 1, and 0). The other big circle has a 3 at the center; it, too, encompasses three numbers (1, 1, and 2).

54

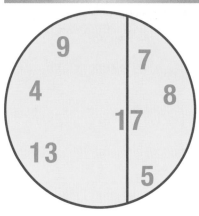

13

55

7	x	4	–	2	+	5	=	31
–	■	x	■	+	■	+	■	
5	–	2	+	4	x	7	=	49
x	■	+	■	x	■	–	■	
2	x	7	–	5	+	4	=	13
+	■	–	■	–	■	x	■	
4	+	5	–	7	x	2	=	4
=	■	=	■	=	■	=	■	
8		10		23		16		

56

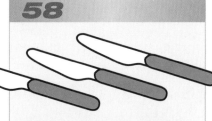

57

3:55 (add 1 hour and 25 minutes each time).

58

Three; one knife weighs as much as two forks, and two knives weigh as much as one spoon. Thus three knives are needed to balance scale c.

59

1. 1,776
2. 7,777
3. 10,701
4. 10,989
5. 2,401
6. 101,010
7. 9,990
8. 494
9. 1,717
10. 7,272
11. 22,222
12. 717

60

A♦	Q♠	K♥	J♣
K♣	J♥	A♠	Q♦
J♠	K♦	Q♣	A♥
Q♥	A♣	J♦	K♠

61

((10 x 6) + 8) x 7 = 476
There are twenty-three other possible solutions.

62

7 – 6 + 5 – 4 = 2
(7 + 6 – 5) ÷ 4 = 2

63

The shortest solution is eighteen moves: 2 to 3, 9 to 4, 10 to 7, 3 to 8, 4 to 2, 7 to 5, 8 to 6, 5 to 10, 6 to 9, 2 to 5, 1 to 6, 6 to 4, 5 to 3, 10 to 8, 4 to 7, 3 to 2, 8 to 1, and 7 to 10.

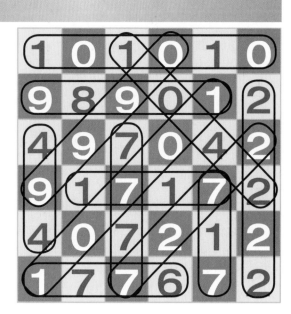

64

Six; two apples weigh as much as five cherries, and nine cherries weigh as much as two bananas. Thus six apples are needed to balance scale c.

65

```
  49747   479351
323 7 0  8 0 2
1 14355  3656016
7 7 3 8  8 3 5 7 8
8179  37513  2056
6 2 8 5  0 2 0 2
1636986  9683726
      5        4
2464093  8757623
1 5 5 7  2 6 2 2
8060  37206  6742
4 9 5 8  8 3 6 0
5829464  75200 0
    4 3 4  5 1 669
  689083  46207
```

66

```
1 9 5 1 9 7 0 9 7 5 9 1
9 7 1 7 9 5 0 1 5 7 9 9
5 0 0 9 0 9 9 0 1 1 9 1
0 9 7 5 9 7 7 9 7 0 7 7
9 5 1 9 1 5 1 0 0 5 0 0
7 9 7 0 5 7 9 9 1 7 9 9
1 1 5 7 0 1 1 0 0 5 1 5
7 7 0 9 9 5 7 0 7 9 1 7
0 0 1 5 9 9 9 5 9 1 7 1
5 7 0 0 1 0 1 7 0 9 5 7
9 9 7 0 5 9 0 7 1 5 7 0
1 1 5 9 1 7 5 9 0 7 9 1
```

67

10¼; there are two series: + 2½ and − 4¼. So we get 2¾, 5¼, 7¾, 10¼, and 13¾, 9½, 5¼.

68

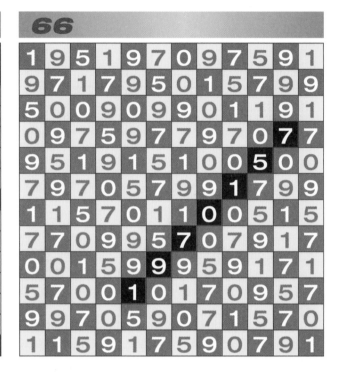

```
            591
        285     306
     134    151     155
   70    64     87     68
 42   28    36    51    17
```

69

29; the rest are a sequence of square numbers minus 1, for example, $2^2 - 1 = 3$, $3^2 - 1 = 8$, $4^2 - 1 = 15$, etc.

70

1. There are six faces to each die, which could land any way up, thus the chance of throwing a double six is one in thirty-six.

2. There are six different combinations of doubles, thus the chance of throwing any double is six in thirty-six, i.e., one in six.

3. Bearing in mind that there are two dice, the chance of throwing both a one and a six is two in thirty-six, i.e., one in eighteen.

4. With six faces to each die, the chance of throwing one particular number is eleven in thirty-six. Throwing two dice does not double your chances of throwing a four, because if you have already thrown one, the second throw is irrelevant, so in one of your six tries you don't need to throw again, i.e., only in 5/6 of the times do you add the 1/6 chance, i.e., 1/6 + 5/6 x 1/6. In other words, the chance of NOT throwing a four is 5/6 x 5/6, i.e., 25/36; thus the chance of throwing at least one four is 1 – 25/36, so 11/36.

71

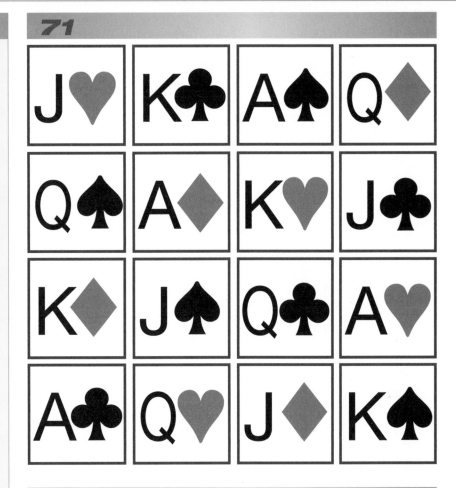

72

((6 + 4) x 9 x 7) − 2 = 628

73

1. 5 and 10
2. a pair of 9s
3. 36; queen (12), king (13), and jack (11)
4. 25; 3 + 8 + 2 + queen (12), and 7 + 4 + ace (1) + king (13)
5. the 4 of clubs
6. 35; 3 + queen (12) + 9 + jack (11)

74

37

75

		9	4	1	9	4		7	0	4	1	1	8
8	6	3		7		8		1		0		7	
6		5	8	5	2	0		3	4	9	5	0	1	2
1		7		6		5		7		6		4		4
7	2	0	6		6	6	7	5	0		2	1	8	6
0		4		4		3		2		1		5		6
3	4	5	8	2	3	2		5	8	1	9	6	7	3
			6						6				
8	7	6	1	7	1	6		2	7	5	2	1	4	6
2		1		6		7		1		4		4		4
5	5	5	9		3	2	1	3	4		8	2	8	2
1		7		9		0		8		6		9		0
8	7	4	4	9	3	4		7	2	0	5	5		0
			1		7	6		1		5		3	7	1
	8	3	7	6	5	6		3	3	8	4	8	

76

Eleven; four spades weigh as much as three hearts, and seven spades weigh as much as three diamonds. Thus eleven spades are needed to balance scale c.

77

Sixteen; six suns weigh as much as one star, and two suns weigh as much as one moon. Thus sixteen suns are needed to balance scale c.

78

1.	4,546
2.	6,534
3.	8,448
4.	10,088
5.	6,500
6.	1,234
7.	60,000
8.	8,020
9.	21,212
10.	3,136
11.	13,006
12.	9,090

79

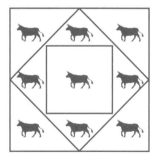

80

−19; there are two series (+19) and (−19): −76, −57, −38, and −19, −27, −46, −65.

81

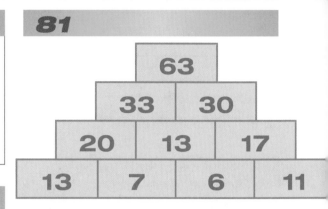

	63	
33		30

20	13	17
13	7	6	11

82

208; the others are divisible by 19.

83

20	+	5	−	11	x	6	=	84
+		x		x		+		
6	+	20	x	5	−	11	=	119
−		+		+		x		
11	−	6	+	20	x	5	=	125
x		−		−		−		
5	x	11	+	6	−	20	=	41
=		=		=		=		
75		95		69		65		

84

Just one; its four sides run diagonally, connecting the midpoints of each side of the larger fence, just touching the corners of the smaller fence.

85

40; starting with 365, add 15 to obtain alternate numbers (so, 365, 380, 395, 410). Then, arrive at the numbers in between by multiplying the number formed by the last two digits by the first digit. So 3 x 65 = 195, and 3 x 80 = 240, etc.

86

87

1:20; (start at 25 minutes past 12 o'clock, then double the number of minutes past 12 each time—i.e., 50 minutes past, 100 minutes past, 200 minutes past...)

88

((3 x 8) + 4) ÷ 2 = 14;   (3 + 8 – 4) x 2 = 14

89

12	2	15	5
1	7	10	16
13	11	6	4
8	14	3	9

90

	6	1	8	8	5		9	3	4	0	6	9
8	4	7		1		7		0		5		2	
7		1	4	3	8	5		3	1	9	9	0	2	4
1		4		2		7		3		6		8		6
6	2	3	2		2	3	5	2	8		3	5	8	6
2		6		8		3		4		5		1		5
5	0	1	8	2	0	6		4	5	0	5	9	7	9
		5								6			
9	7	2	6	7	0	8		1	3	5	3	7	4	5
1		4		5		1		3		8		0		9
5	3	5	8		7	7	5	7	6		2	7	7	9
1		5		1		1		9		7		0		5
3	1	2	9	8	1	5		9	2	5	2	8		6
	9		0		3		6		1		7	7	0
7	8	4	5	2	9		3	8	9	2	3	

91

8	6	4	3	7	1
8	0	0	8	3	1
0	6	4	7	4	1
8	0	9	4	5	1
8	6	0	3	6	3
2	0	4	4	4	4

1.	26,973	7.	13,800
2.	3,456	8.	60,606
3.	3,630	9.	1,111
4.	4,000	10.	4,400
5.	88,088	11.	1,734
6.	4,444	12.	404

92

A maximum of fourteen (or fifteen if you include the square on which you start); there's no way of visiting the whole board, no matter which route you take.

93

37; there are twenty-one spots on each die, thus a total of sixty-three spots on the three dice. Since twenty-six spots are visible, the total number of spots on the sides that are not visible amounts to thirty-seven.

94

59

95

7,359; each number in the sequence (except the first and the odd one out) is obtained by taking the previous number and adding its two central numbers to it; e.g., 7,246 + 24 = 7,270.

96

(4 x 3) − 1 − 2 = 9
((4 + 3) ÷ 1) + 2 = 9
((4 + 3) x 1) + 2 = 9

97

98

99

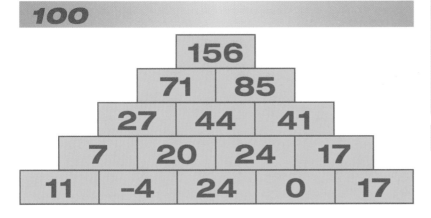

```
                184
            54      130
         37     17     113
      24     13      4     109
```

100

```
                156
             71     85
          27    44    41
        7    20    24    17
     11   -4    24    0    17
```

101

```
 3 0 1 7 1   9 9 3 1 3 6
2 0 8   0   9   2   1   8
5   9 2 6 5 1   9 5 4 6 2 8 2
8   3   7   1   6   8   2   0
2 5 2 0   1 1 2 4 6   9 1 8 1
3   3   4   6   8   7   7   5
1 0 6 4 3 6 0   2 0 3 1 1 8 4
          6           3
6 6 5 9 8 9 7   4 4 1 1 2 3 7
9   1   1   2   6   2   2   8
4 0 5 4   5 2 7 3 4   7 9 8 5
1   0   8   1   6   5   6   9
8 6 0 3 9 4 3   8 2 3 6 2   8
    3   8   5   3   2   8 4 4
    6 2 3 2 6 1   5 3 9 3 1
```

102

Each line must total twelve, thus (allowing for possible rotations and reflections) this is one possible solution:

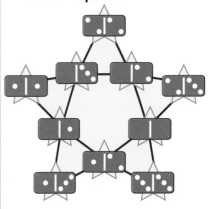

103

2,868; reverse the previous number and add 1 to the same digit each time (which starts out as the 4 of the 2,468).

104

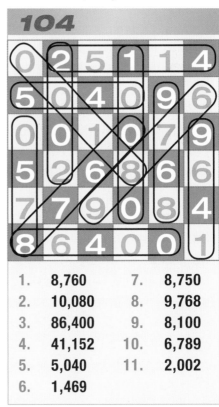

1. 8,760	7. 8,750
2. 10,080	8. 9,768
3. 86,400	9. 8,100
4. 41,152	10. 6,789
5. 5,040	11. 2,002
6. 1,469	

105

1:55; advance the previous clock by the amount shown on the clock before that; i.e., effectively add the previous two clocks together, so 1:10 and 2:05 would mean 110 plus 205, giving 315, or 3:15, the time shown on clock c, and so on.

106

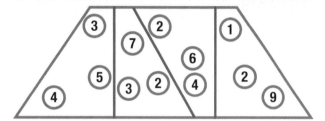

107

819; 819 is a square number followed by its square root, i.e., $9^2 = 81$, while all the other numbers are cube numbers followed by their cube roots. For example, 3,437, where $7^3 = 343$.

108

30; Angelica can see the top faces of all three dice, thus a total of fifteen spots. The opposite sides of a die add up to seven. On the furthest left die, the side face Angelica can see has one spot. On the central die, the side face Angelica can see has five spots. On the furthest right die, the side face Angelica can see has four spots. On the bottom face of the furthest right die there is one spot, so the end face of this die (invisible to you) has either two or five spots. If this end face has two spots, then the total number of spots Angelica can see is twenty-seven. But Angelica can see more spots than you, and you would be able to see twenty-nine. So the end face Angelica can see must have five spots. Thus Angelica can see a total of fifteen spots on the top faces, ten spots on the side faces, and five on the end face, so a combined total of thirty spots.

109

110

Ten routes; two clear runs and eight that go through one star.

111

15	−	4	x	9	+	14	=	113
+		x		−		+		
14	+	15	−	4	x	9	=	225
x		−		x		x		
9	x	14	+	15	−	4	=	137
−		+		+		−		
4	x	9	+	14	−	15	=	35
=		=		=		=		
257		55		89		77		

112

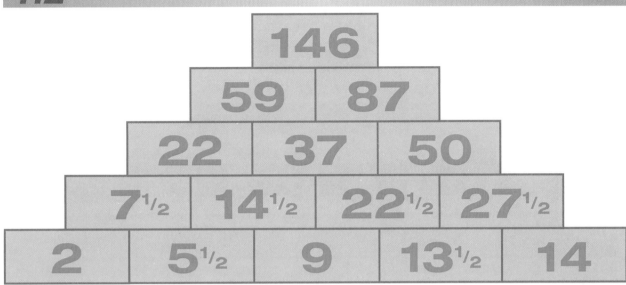

146

59   87

22   37   50

$7^{1/2}$ $14^{1/2}$ $22^{1/2}$ $27^{1/2}$

2    $5^{1/2}$ 9 $13^{1/2}$ 14

113

4:40; in each case each hand moves forward a number of places determined by the number of letters in its last position. So, for example, the hour hand of the first clock shows one. Because this has three letters, it moves three positions to point to four on the next clock. Similarly, the minute hand of the first clock shows five, so on the next clock it shows nine because it has moved on four positions (i.e., the number of letters in five), and so on.

114

13	3	16	2
8	10	5	11
1	15	4	14
12	6	9	7

115

$((5 + 19) \div 6) \div 1 = 4$
$((5 + 19) \div 6) \times 1 = 4$

116

1. Green
2. Music 197
3. 11:15 P.M.
4. Sports 1532
5. News 350
6. Green

117

	2	2	7	9	9		2	1	9	0	6	9	
8	8	5		0		1		3		6		0	
8		4	3	4	1	3		7	6	5	1	3	4	1
3		1		4		3		8		8		2		0
4	8	5	4		8	3	7	2	9		3	9	1	6
7		0		9		8		5		3		2		8
3	1	3	0	4	4	2		7	6	1	7	6	2	1
					0					6				
6	3	5	1	9	1	5		1	1	6	6	8	7	1
8		2		6		5		5		8		2		9
5	1	9	5		7	1	3	3	4		8	6	3	8
2		8		6		1		1		2		5		9
9	7	1	5	9	4	4		5	2	8	4	2		5
		9		0		5		9		1		5	1	3
	7	8	7	2	6	5		6	3	2	0	7		

118

$(((7 \times 7) - 4) \times 5) \times 4 = 900$ There are four other possible solutions.

119

Six; one square and two circles weigh as much as one triangle; thus two squares weigh as much as one triangle, as do four circles. Therefore two circles weigh as much as one square, so we need another four circles (equivalent to two squares) plus two circles in scale c. Thus six circles are needed to balance scale c.

120

4,805; in all the others multiply the first and third digits to obtain the number formed by the second and fourth digits, for example, 4 x 5 = 20. With 4,805, multiply the second and fourth digits to obtain the number formed by the first and third digits.

121

The diagonals have no 5s, so in column 5 the second face down is a 3. In row 2, the 5 is in column 3. In column 3, the 1 is in row 4. The top right diagonal totals 23 (intro), so is 6, 3, 6, 1, 6, 1. Column 3 has a 4 in row 5 and a 6 in row 6. Column 6 has a 1 in row 3, so must have a 5 in row 4. Column 5 has a 6 in row 4. For a total of 17 (intro), the top left diagonal is (by elimination) 4, 2, 3, 4, 1, 3. Thus in row 5, column 6 is 2. Column 1 is thus 4, 6, 5, 2, 3, 1, and (by elimination) the solution is:

4	1	2	3	5	6
6	2	5	1	3	4
5	4	3	6	2	1
2	3	1	4	6	5
3	6	4	5	1	2
1	5	6	2	4	3

122

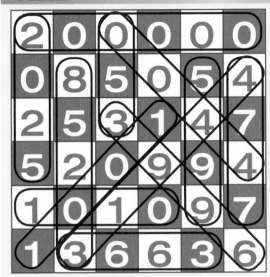

1. 31,944
2. 30,258
3. 3,996
4. 9,945
5. 2,025
6. 200,000
7. 4,400
8. 3,663
9. 1,001
10. 350
11. 1,010
12. 4,747

123

One; put the smaller box inside the larger (i.e., moving the 9 coin), so the big box effectively holds all the coins.

124

1,718; to find the next number in the series, add the two middle numbers to the previous number: e.g., 1,594 + 59 = 1,653.

125

1:00; (the minute hand moves +1, +2, +3... positions forward; the hour hand is similar but moves backward instead).

126

$(5 \times \frac{1}{4}) - \frac{1}{4} + 6 = 8\frac{1}{4}$

$((5 + \frac{1}{2}) \times \frac{1}{4}) \times 6 = 8\frac{1}{4}$

127

Note: The 9/1 tile has been inverted to become 1/6!

128

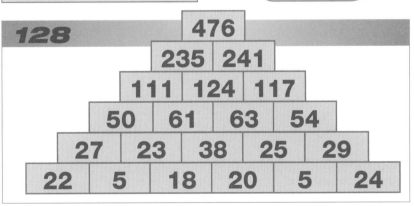

129

2,222; add each number to its reverse to get the next number: e.g., 605 + 506 = 1,111.

130

18; add the number of spots on the three visible faces of each die, then do the same for the invisible faces of each die. Now deduct the lower total from the higher total and multiply that answer by two.

131

Whichever way you place the dominoes, the 0-6 is always left over.

132

63

133

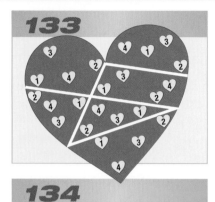

134

148; add all the previous digits to the last number, including the digits of the last number itself. So start with 23 + 2 + 3 = 28, and work up to 98 + 9 + 8 + 6 + 5 + 4 + 3 + 2 + 8 + 2 + 3 = 148.

135

2; in each case the hour hand moves forward one hour. The minute hand moves forward by the total given by adding the number to which the hour hand in the previous clock points to the number to which the minute hand points. So the minute hand of clock b is moved by four places (1 + 3 of clock a) to show 2:35; clock c shows 3:20 because the minute hand has moved on another nine places (2 + 7 of clock b), etc.

136

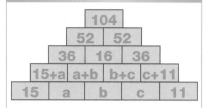

The top three levels are easy to fill in. Next, replace the three unknowns with a, b, and c. This gives us these three equations:

$36 = (15 + a) + (a + b)$
hence $2a + b = 21$

$16 = (a + b) + (b + c)$
hence $a + 2b + c = 16$

$36 = (b + c) + (c + 11)$
hence $b + 2c = 25$

Adding the first and last equation together gives $2a + 2b + 2c = 46$ hence $a + b + c = 23$

Comparing this to the middle equation shows that b must be −7, since it has another b but the total is 7 lower. Now that we know b = −7, it's easy to see that a = 14 and c = 16 from the other equations. The rest of the pyramid can now be completed:

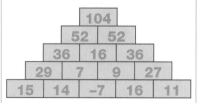

137

64; the other numbers are $4^2 - 1$, $5^2 - 1$, etc.

138

139

$((9 \times 7) + (75 \div 25))$ $\times (10 + 4) = 924$ There are ten other possible solutions.

140

Domino 4/0 (with the 4 at the top); the total number of dots on one domino equals the top of the domino to its right.

141

5,464; each number is obtained by taking the previous number and adding the first and last digit, i.e., 5,431 + (5 + 1 = 6) = 5,437. So 5,464 should be 5,463 for the rest of the sequence to make sense.

142

9,158; take the number formed by the odd digits in the correct order from the previous number multiplied by the number formed by the digits of the even numbers. So, 75,634 produces 753 x 64 = 48,192.

143

1. 5,040
2. 39,483
3. 9,768
4. 13,534
5. 48,400
6. 2,596
7. 9,797
8. 8,888
9. 4,400
10. 7,470
11. 38,416

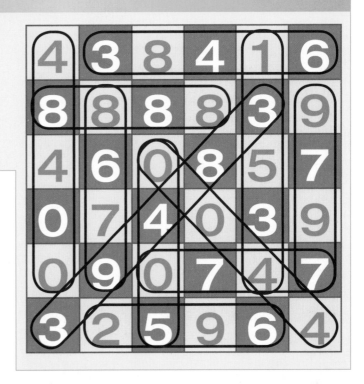

144

((24 ÷ 6) x 9) ÷ 2 = 18

((24 x 6) ÷ 9) + 2 = 18

(24 − 6 − 9) x 2 = 18

145

None; just move the tiles horizontally and vertically instead.

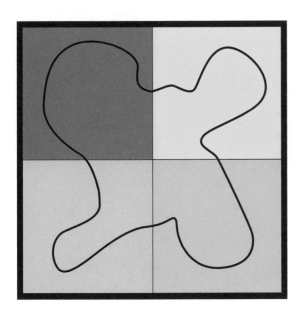

146

ACKNOWLEDGMENTS ✪ NUMERIC PUZZLES

✪ Puzzle contributors
Contributors are listed next to the numbers of the puzzles they created.

✪ David Bodycombe
Puzzles 1, 3, 5, 10, 14, 15, 17, 18, 28, 30, 31, 38, 39, 47, 53, 57, 60, 61, 62, 63, 68, 71, 72, 81, 84, 87, 88, 89, 92, 96, 99, 100, 195, 110, 112, 113, 114, 115, 118, 123, 125, 126, 127, 128, 135, 136, 139, 144, 145, 146

✪ Guy Campbell
Puzzles 6, 8, 36, 45, 59, 78, 91, 104, 122, 143

✪ Philip Carter and Ken Russell
Puzzles 16, 19, 22, 27, 29, 34, 43, 44, 48, 52, 54, 67, 69, 74, 80, 82, 85, 94, 95, 103, 107, 109, 120, 124, 129, 132, 134, 137, 141, 142

✪ Probyn Puzzles
Puzzles 2, 9, 12, 32, 55, 65, 75, 83, 90, 101, 111, 117

✪ Puzzlemakers
Puzzles 4, 7, 11, 13, 20, 21, 23, 24, 25, 26, 33, 35, 37, 40, 41, 42, 46, 49, 50, 51, 56, 58, 64, 66, 70, 73, 76, 77, 79, 86, 93, 97, 98, 102, 106, 108, 116, 119, 121, 130, 131, 133, 138, 140

Numerical Puzzles was commissioned, edited, designed, and produced by:
Librios Publishing Ltd., 21 Catherine Street, London WC2B 5JS, United Kingdom
Managing Director: Hal Robinson
Editor: Alison Moore **Project Editor:** Marilyn Inglis **Art Editor:** Keith Miller
Designers: Michael Chapman, Austin Taylor, Evelyn Bercott **Copy Editor:** Sarah Barlow